SPANISH
GCSE Grade Booster

A. E. Henderson

Schofield & Sims Ltd.

© 1991 Schofield & Sims Ltd.

All rights reserved.
No part of this publication may be
reproduced, stored in a retrieval system, or
transmitted, in any form, or by any means,
electronic, mechanical, photocopying,
recording or otherwise, without the prior
permission of Schofield & Sims Ltd.

0 7217 4619 5

First printed 1991

Schofield & Sims Ltd.
Dogley Mill
Fenay Bridge
Huddersfield
HD8 0NQ
England

Typeset by Ocean, Leeds
Printed in Great Britain by the Alden Press, Oxford

Contents

	Introduction	4
1	**An Exchange Is Arranged**	5
	Form filling - friendly letters - describing people - personal 'a' - present tense - radical changing verbs - adjectives	
2	**First Day in Spain**	17
	Daily routine - reflexive verbs - asking questions - the Tourist Office - asking the way - giving directions - 'ser' or 'estar'? - describing where you live - town or country? - Spain is different - advice on reading test - signs	
3	**Planning a Party**	31
	Inviting - asking permission - forbidding - requests - accepting - refusing - apologies - arranging to meet - introductions - negative words - seasons, dates and numbers - time - 'for' with time - continuous present and gerund - 'to meet' - free time - bullfights	
4	**Talking About the Future**	44
	Jobs - future tenses - school - likes and dislikes ('gustar') - expressing approval, disapproval and surprise - formal letters - applying for jobs - 'and' and 'or' - avoiding subjunctive - advice on listening test	
5	**A Day Out**	56
	Filling station - breakdowns - transport - buying a rail ticket - countries - 'to have just' - necessity - preterite tense - which past tense?	
6	**Booking a Camp Site or Hotel**	67
	Letter to a hotel - holidays - 'to stay' - weather forecast with practice answer - hot and cold - phrases with 'tener' - skiing - adverbs - imperfect tense - continuous imperfect tense	
7	**A Chapter of Accidents**	81
	Illness - the dentist - accidents - comparisons - perfect tense - imperatives (commands)	
8	**Using Public Services**	93
	Banks - post office - telephone - getting things done - lost and found - pronouns - 'poder', 'saber', 'conocer' - tenses with emotions - tenses with 'querer', 'saber', 'poder' - pluperfect tense	
9	**A Shopping Trip**	104
	Buying things - returning purchases - quantities - complaints - advice on messages - making yourself understood - polite phrases - 'lo' + adjective or adverb - conditional tense	
10	**Farewell to Spain**	115
	Eating out - thanking people - expressing pleasure - complaints in restaurants - 'para' or 'por'? - phrases with 'por' - 'sitting' - future perfect tense - conditional perfect tense - probability - advice on the speaking test	
	Index of Grammar	126
	Index of Topics	128

Introduction

Using the Book

This GCSE Spanish Grade Booster is not a course book but a revision book. All the main topics and all the basic grammar you need for a good grade in GCSE are covered. There are also helpful suggestions on how to tackle different kinds of question, such as writing letters, taking messages or preparing your spoken role-play.

You can begin with Chapter 1 and work through steadily to the end. You will then have thoroughly revised all you need to know for GCSE. Or you can select topics or language areas that you feel less confident about and concentrate on revising them.

Each chapter begins with a story in Spanish about the experiences of an English girl visiting her exchange partner in Seville. This provides reading practice, and useful phrases to learn for the writing and speaking tests. Every chapter concentrates on a particular topic, and revises specific points of grammar. The grammar is not exhaustive, but deals with those aspects likely to cause problems. There is an alphabetical index of points revised at the end of the book.

It is assumed that the language needed for GCSE has already been covered, so a variety of tenses is used from the beginning and the Spanish does not get progressively more difficult throughout the book. You are not expected to understand every word of the authentic material used in GCSE, so quite difficult idioms have sometimes been deliberately used in the reading sections.

Remember: GCSE is marked positively, i.e. points are given for what you *know* and what you *can* say and understand.

Using the Cassette

There is a cassette with the book, and at the end of every chapter there are a listening practice (with answers) and two speaking practice exercises, with gaps for you to provide your part of the role-play. Possible answers are also recorded. Each section on the cassette is related to the topic for the chapter it follows, and in the speaking practice there is always one easy role-play and one more suitable for Higher Level.

Acknowledgement

The author would like to thank Dr Rafael Sala of Bradford University for a helpful and very careful reading of the manuscript.

1 An Exchange Is Arranged

This chapter revises talking about yourself and your family. There is an example of a form to fill in and advice on writing informal letters. The grammar revised is the personal 'a', the present tense, radical changing verbs, and adjectives.

Elena Decides to Do an Exchange

Elena llegó corriendo a casa, abrió la puerta del cuarto de estar y gritó:
—Mamá, papá, ¿dónde estáis?
—¿Pero qué te pasa, niña?
Elena les mostró el papel que traía del Instituto, y les explicó que su profesor de inglés les había dicho que cada año el Instituto hacía un intercambio con un colegio inglés, en el norte de Inglaterra. Los ingleses venían en abril, y pasaban tres semanas en Sevilla. En julio los españoles iban a Bradford. Los que querían participar en el intercambio tenían que devolver el formulario de solicitud lo antes posible.
—Tú no quieres ir, porque te vas a Marbella con los primos en julio, ¿verdad?
—Oye, papá. Los tíos pasan dos meses en la costa. Puedo veranear en Marbella en agosto, o espero hasta el año que viene. Ya sabéis que saqué una mala nota en inglés el mes pasado. Dejadme ir a Inglaterra. Todos mis amigos van. Vamos a pasarlo bomba.
—Exacto. Eso es lo que temo.
—Papá, me estás tomando el pelo. Dime que puedo.
—Sí, si es que te apetece tanto.
—Gracias. Eres un ángel.
—Siempre te sales con la tuya.

Vocabulary

¿qué te pasa? what's the matter?	**pasarlo bomba** to have a whale of a time
hacer un intercambio to do an exchange	**eso es lo que temo** that's what I'm afraid of
devolver to give back	**me estás tomando el pelo** you're pulling my leg
el formulario de solicitud application form	**si es que te apetece tanto** if you want to so much
lo antes posible as soon as possible	**siempre te sales con la tuya** you always get your own way
saqué una mala nota I got a bad grade	

Filling in a Form

```
                    Solicitud de intercambio

Nombre: Mª Elena                  Nacionalidad: española
Apellidos: Martínez García        Lugar de nacimiento: Sevilla
Dirección: Avenida de Cuba 91, 3º D   Fecha de nacimiento: 1 de octubre de 1974
           Sevilla 41011          Profesión del padre: gerente
Número de teléfono: 95 4452638    Profesión de la madre: ama de casa
¿Vives en un piso? Sí             Hermanos (con edad):
         una casa adosada?            José Luis - 21 años
         un chalet?                   Javier - 18 años
         un pueblo?                   Ana - 10 años
         una urbanización?        ¿Cuántos dormitorios tiene? cuatro
         el centro ciudad?        ¿Cuántos cuartos de baño? dos
¿Tienes animales en casa?         ¿Habitación individual para el amigo? } puede
  Un canario                      ¿O tiene que compartir?                } elegir
                                  ¿Tiene calefacción central?
                                       Sí
Carácter: abierta, sincera, sociable
¿Qué intereses tienes?            ¿Eres socio de algún club?
  jugar al tenis, nadar,            Sí, del club deportivo del Pinar
  leer
¿Cómo pasas tu tiempo libre?      ¿Cuánta libertad te permiten tus padres?
  Salgo con amigos, veo la televisión,  Lo normal para mi edad. Siempre saben
  hago deporte                      dónde estoy y con quién.
Firma del alumno:                 Firma del padre:

  Elena Pérez G.                     Rafael Martínez Morales
```

Vocabulary

el apellido surname (Spaniards have two)	**el lugar de nacimiento** place of birth
el estado civil marital status	**la dirección** address
casado, -da married	**las señas** name and address
soltero, -ra single	**compartir** to share
parado, -da unemployed	**el chalet** detached house
jubilado, -da retired	**la casa adosada** terraced house
la calefacción central central heating	**una urbanización** new development
el domicilio home address	

Elena Writes to Her Exchange

Sevilla, 2 de febrero de 1990

Querida Sarah:

¡Hola! Me llamo Elena y tengo dieciséis años. Nuestro profesor de inglés acaba de darme tu dirección porque vamos a hacer un un intercambio. Me hace mucha ilusión porque es la primera vez que visito Inglaterra.

Bueno, te voy a describir mi familia. Somos seis en casa: mis padres, mi hermano mayor José Luis, Javier, que tiene dieciocho años, Ana, mi hermana menor, y yo. Mi padre se llama Rafael y es gerente de una fábrica; mi madre se llama Conchita y no trabaja, es ama de casa.

José Luis tiene veintiún años y estudia Filosofía y Letras en la Universidad. Es alto y guapo. Es muy alegre y siempre le gusta estar con amigos. Javier no quiere ir a la Universidad y al terminar va a buscar trabajo. Es un chico muy serio, muy formal, pero tiene muchos amigos. Le encanta el fútbol y forma parte de un equipo del instituto. Es hincha del Betis y no se pierde nunca un partido.

Ana tiene once años, es bajita, gordita, tiene el pelo rubio y rizado como mi madre y los ojos grises. Es muy viva, impulsiva, traviesa y lista... ¡y algo mimada!

¿Y yo? Pues soy alta, delgada, y tengo el pelo castaño y muy largo y los ojos oscuros. Soy más tranquila que Ana y un poco tímida con la gente que no conozco, pero juego mucho al tenis y me gusta la natación. Soy socia de un club deportivo donde podemos practicar muchos deportes y montar a caballo si quieres. En mis ratos libres me gusta leer, ver la TV o salir con mis amigos. De vez en cuando voy a una discoteca con mis hermanos.

No tenemos animales en casa, pero sí tenemos un canario. Me gustaría tener un perro pero mi madre les tiene mucho miedo.

Ya está bien de hablar de mí, cuéntame algo de tu familia y de tus aficiones. Espero tu llegada con mucha ilusión. Escríbeme pronto.

Un abrazo muy fuerte

Elena

Vocabulary

me hace mucha ilusión I'm very excited	**el Betis** one of Seville's two football clubs
espero con mucha ilusión I'm looking forward to	**el socio, la socia** member
es gerente de una fábrica he's the manager of a factory	**en mis ratos libres** in my free time
es ama de casa she's a housewife	**de vez en cuando** occasionally
Filosofía y Letras Arts course at university	**pero sí tenemos** but we do have
el BUP equivalent of GCSE	**basta de mí** that's enough of me
el hincha fan	**cuéntame algo de** tell me something about

Writing Personal Letters

Address
Do not write your address at the top of the letter. It goes on the back of the envelope.

Date
At the top right-hand side of the letter, put the town you are writing from, followed by the date <u>on the same line</u>.

e.g. *Bristol, 9 de agosto de 1991.*

Beginning
Use *Querida* for a girl, *Querido* for a boy, followed by the first name:
   Querida Begoña: *Querido Pablo:*
Use *Queridos* to more than one person:
   Queridos papá y mamá:
- Spaniards use a colon (:) after the name where we use a comma.

Content
Remember to include everything the question asks you to say. Tick off the points on the question paper as you write them. Do NOT copy words or phrases from the examination paper. Do NOT repeat words or phrases within your own letter, unless it's unavoidable.

Ending
Usually:
   Un abrazo
   Un fuerte abrazo } Love from . . .

Describing People

Boys may prefer:
Un saludo cordial de ⎫
Tu amigo ⎭ Regards from . . .

Sign your first name on the line below.

Describing People

Use *ser* with most adjectives, but use *tener . . . años* to say how old someone is. Hair and eyes are often described with *tener*.

e.g. *Mi tío tiene los ojos y el pelo morenos, pero mis primos tienen el pelo castaño y los ojos azules.*
My uncle has dark eyes and dark hair, but my cousins have light brown hair and blue eyes.

Make sure you can describe the appearance and character of yourself, your best friend, your family, your teacher and any pets you have. Use the feminine form of adjectives for girls or women.

Useful Descriptions

mi profesor es	my teacher is	**lleva gafas**	he wears glasses
guapo	handsome	**mi madre es**	my mother is
feo	ugly	**pelirroja**	red-haired
calvo	bald	**rubia**	blonde
tranquilo	calm	**cana**	grey-haired
tímido	shy	**tiene**	she has
trabajador	hardworking	**el pelo liso**	straight hair
lleva bigote	he has a moustache	**tiene**	she has
una barba	a beard	**el pelo rizado**	curly hair

Mi profesor es muy trabajador.

mi sobrino es listo	my nephew is clever		
tonto	silly	**formal**	reliable
amable	kind	**servicial**	helpful
abierto	frank	**deportista**	sporty
cariñoso	affectionate	**perezoso**	lazy
mimado	spoilt	**sensible**	sensitive
travieso	naughty	**sensato**	sensible

The Personal 'a'

If the object of the verb is a person, the word *a* must be used in front of it. It can be used before a name, before a noun (e.g. *hermana*, *médico*), or before a pronoun (e.g. *ése*, *quien*, *Vd.*).

e.g. *Conocí a tu amigo alemán anoche.*   I met your German friend last night.
No ve a nadie los domingos.   He never sees anybody on Sundays.

- Personal *a* is never used after *tener* or *hay*.
  e.g. *Tengo tres tías.* I have three aunts.
  Hay un señor aquí que quiere hablar con papá. There's a gentleman here who wants to talk to Father.

The Two Ways of Saying 'You'

a) When talking to someone older, whom you don't know well (for example, a friend's father or a shop assistant), use *Vd.* This is pronounced, and sometimes written, *usted*. Use *Vd.* for one person, and *Vds.* (*ustedes*) for more than one.

Vd. takes the same verb as 'he'.
Vds. takes the same verb as 'they'.

Vds. comen muchos cacahuetes.

e.g. *Juan come muchas manzanas.* Juan eats a lot of apples.
Vd. come muchas manzanas. You (singular, polite) eat a lot of apples.
Pilar y Jorge comen cacahuetes. Pilar and Jorge eat peanuts.
Vds. comen cacahuetes. You (plural, polite) eat peanuts.

b) When talking to people of your own age, friends and members of the family, use *tú* to one person, and *vosotros* (masculine) or *vosotras* (feminine) to more than one. There is a special part of the verb for both *tú* and *vosotros*.

e.g. *Vives en Valladolid.* You (one person, familiar, *tú*) live in Valladolid.
Vivís en Valladolid. You (plural, familiar, *vosotros*) live in Valladolid.

● You will have to use both *tú* and *Vd.* in the examination. If you use someone's first name, use *tú*. Whichever you choose, keep to either *tú* or *Vd.* throughout that question.

The Present Tense

The endings of verbs are important because the subject pronouns (I, you, etc.) are usually left out. Someone who said 'I goes' or 'she speak' would still be understood in English; but if you say *hablas* when you mean *habla*, there is nothing to show you mean 'she' and not 'you'.

There are three main groups of regular verbs, called *-ar*, *-er* or *-ir* verbs from the ending of the infinitive. All form the present tense by removing *-ar*, *-er* or *-ir* and adding endings as follows.

-ar *comprar*, to buy		-er *comer*, to eat		-ir *escribir*, to write	
compr|*o*	I buy, I do buy, I am buying	*com*|*o*	I eat, etc.	*escrib*|*o*	I write, etc.
compr|*as*	you (*tú*) buy	*com*|*es*		*escrib*|*es*	
compr|*a*	s/he, you(*Vd.*) buy(s)	*com*|*e*		*escrib*|*e*	
compr|*amos*	we buy	*com*|*emos*		*escrib*|*imos*	
compr|*áis*	you (*vosotros*) buy	*com*|*éis*		*escrib*|*ís*	
compr|*an*	they, you (*Vds.*) buy	*com*|*en*		*escrib*|*en*	

● The *-er* and *-ir* verbs have the same endings except for 'we' and 'you' (*vosotros*). Irregular verbs must be learnt individually from a grammar book.

Radical Changing Verbs

These verbs change the last vowel immediately before -*ar*, -*er* or -*ir* in the present tense, except in the *nosotros* (we) and *vosotros* (you, plural familiar) forms. *E* changes to *ie*; *o* to *ue*, and *u* to *ue*. Some -*ir* verbs change to only one letter, *e* to *i*, or *o* to *u*.

You can't tell which verbs change the root vowel — you just have to learn them.

Here are two examples.

atravesar, to cross *e → ie*	*atravieso* *atraviesas* *atraviesa* *atravesamos* *atravesáis* *atraviesan*	*reír*, to laugh *e → i*	*río* *ríes* *ríe* *reímos* *reís* *ríen*

Adjectives

Adjectives (big, red, young, etc.) describe a noun.

1. Feminine

If the masculine ends in -*o*, there will be a feminine form in -*a*, which you must use to describe feminine nouns. If the masculine adjective does NOT end in -*o*, the feminine form is the same as the masculine.

e.g. *Un edificio blanco con una puerta negra.*   A white building with a black door.

El traje es azul y la camisa es azul también.   The suit is blue and the shirt is blue, too.

● When the same adjective describes both a masculine and a feminine noun, use the masculine form.

e.g. *Pisos y casas nuevos.*   New flats and houses.

2. Plural

If the adjective describes more than one thing, it must be plural.
Add -*s* if the adjective ends in a vowel.
Add -*es* if it ends in a consonant.

The same rule applies to the plural of nouns.

e.g. *una chica guapa*   a pretty girl
tres chicas guapas   three pretty girls
un montón enorme de naranjas   a huge heap of oranges
montones enormes de naranjas   huge heaps of oranges

3. Nationality

ALL adjectives of nationality and regional origin have a feminine form, whether the masculine singular ends in -o or not.

e.g. *inglés, ingleses; inglesa, inglesas*
español, españoles; española, españolas

4. Short Forms

Some adjectives lose -o before a masculine singular noun, but NOT if they come after the noun, are feminine or plural.

a, one	*uno*	*un gato* but *una vaca*, *unos gatos* (a cow, some cats)
some	*alguno*	*algún periódico* but *alguna revista*, *algunos periódicos* (some magazine, some newspapers)
no	*ninguno*	*ningún pan* but *ninguna idea* (no bread, no idea) rarely used in plural
first	*primero*	*el primer año* but *la primera semana*, *los primeros años* (the first week, the first years)
third	*tercero*	*el tercer piso* but *la tercera vez* (the third floor, the third time) rarely used in plural
good	*bueno*	*un buen bebé* but *una buena niña*, *buenos bebés* (a good girl, good babies)
bad	*malo*	*un mal hombre* but *una mala mujer*, *malos hombres* (a bad woman, bad men)

Un mal hombre.

¿Una mala mujer?

- *Grande* becomes *gran* before ANY singular noun.
    e.g. *un gran rey* but *los grandes reyes*, the great kings
    una gran reina but *las grandes reinas*, the great queens

Adjectives

5. Position

Adjectives normally follow the noun they describe, but some common ones come in front.

bueno, -na good	**cada** each
malo, -la bad	(does not agree)
pequeño, -ña small	**bastante** enough
joven young	**demasiado, -da** too many
viejo, -ja old	**mucho, -cha** many
próximo, -ma next	**otro, otra** (an)other
primero, -ra first	**poco, -ca** few
(and all ordinal numbers)	**semejante** such
alguno, -na some	**tal** such
ninguno, -na no	**todo, -da** every
último, -ma last	

Some adjectives have a different meaning when they come before the noun.

antiguo	an *antiguo* alumno a former pupil	un castillo *antiguo* an ancient castle
nuevo	un *nuevo* coche a new (different) car (could be second-hand)	un coche *nuevo* a brand new car
pobre	¡el *pobre* niño! the poor child! (sorry for him)	un niño *pobre* a poor child (not rich)
grande	un *gran* cuadro a great picture	un cuadro *grande* a big picture

6. Possessive Adjectives

Possessive adjectives come before the noun and agree with <u>what is owned</u>, not with the <u>owner</u>, so that <u>his</u> and <u>her</u> are identical in Spanish, but will be masculine, feminine or plural according to <u>what belongs</u> to him or her.

    e.g. *nuestra madre, nuestro hermano y nuestros amigos* our mother, our brother and our friends

They are:
mi, mis   my
tu, tus   your (familiar, singular)
su, sus   his, her, your, their

nuestro,-tra; nuestros,-tras   our
vuestro,-tra; vuestros,-tras   your (familiar, plural)
Only *nuestro* and *vuestro* have a feminine form.
- <u>su</u> *padre* can mean   <u>sus</u> *padres* can mean
    his father   his parents
    her father   her parents
    their father   their parents
    your (*Vd.* or *Vds.*) father   your (*Vd.*, *Vds.*) parents

Less common are *mío*, *tuyo* and *suyo*. They are used AFTER the noun, and mean 'of mine', 'of yours', etc. *Nuestro* and *vuestro* can be used in the same way.

   e.g. *un amigo mío*   a friend of mine
      unas primas vuestras   some (female) cousins of yours
      ¡esas ideas suyas!   those ideas of his/hers/theirs/yours!

Listening Practice

For this section you need the cassette. Listen carefully to the instructions at the beginning of the tape.

Here is the Spanish alphabet:
a b c ch d e f g h i j k l ll m n ñ o p q r rr s t u v w x y z

Practise spelling in Spanish.

1. The names of four countries will be spelt. Write down the names of the countries.
2. Here are three photographs. Listen to the description, and decide which photograph is being described.

3. In your Spanish friend's school you overhear two boys talking about an exchange visit.
    a) Where did Lucas go two years ago?
    b) What was his opinion of it?

    c)   Give three reasons why Diego thinks Lucas should go on the exchange.
    d)   Why doesn't Lucas want to go? (two reasons)
    e)   What does Lucas agree to do?

Answers:
1. (a) España (b) Venezuela (c) Bélgica (d) Inglaterra.
2. C.
3. (a) Ireland (b) He didn't like it (c) He's studying for the bachillerato this year; can practise his English; will get good grades; English teacher will find him a nice family (d) He doesn't like English food; his girlfriend will be angry (e) Talk to his parents and see what they say.

Speaking Practice

Hints on tackling this part of the examination are on page 122. There are two role-plays, recorded with gaps for you to say your role. A possible answer is recorded after the gap, with a pause for you to repeat it if your own answer was not satisfactory. Use *tú* for friends, *Vd.* for other adults.

1. Your Spanish friend is asking you about your family. She begins:
    How many brothers have you got?
    a)   Say you have two, John who is eighteen and Peter who is twelve.
    Are they good-looking?
    b)   Tell her John is tall, with grey eyes. Peter is thin and blond.
    What are they like? Are they nice?
    c)   Say that John is shy but very sporty. Peter is cheerful and likes to go out with friends.

2. (Higher level) When you were taking your Spanish friend's dog for a walk, it ran away. You ask a policeman if he's seen it. You begin:
    a)   Attract his attention; then tell him you've lost your friend's dog.
    What's the dog like?
    b)   Tell him it's called Bob, and is small and black and has long ears.
    It will probably come home eventually.
    c)   Explain that you're worried because the family are very fond of the dog.
    Do you think it's been stolen?
    d)   Say you think it's possible. It's very affectionate and has no fear of strangers.

2 | First Day in Spain

This chapter will help you to talk about your daily routine and household chores. It will help you to describe where you live, talk about Spain, ask the way, give directions and understand common signs. It revises reflexive verbs, how to ask questions, and whether to use 'ser' or 'estar'. There is also some advice on how to tackle the reading test.

Sarah's First Day

Sarah se despertó a las ocho. Se levantó, se duchó, se vistió, se peinó y luego abrió la contraventana. ¡Qué sorpresa más agradable! Tenía un pequeño balcón, con macetas de flores. Daba al patio, donde se veía a la portera tendiendo ropa. El sol brillaba; hacía calor.

Se dirigió hacia la cocina donde la esperaba Elena y toda la familia. Los había conocido todos ayer en el aeropuerto de Sevilla, donde la habían recogido a las diez de la noche. Después de desayunar, Sarah se volvió hacia la señora de Martínez y le dijo:

—¿Puedo ayudarla? ¿Quito la mesa?

—No, no, Sarah, gracias. Hoy vas a descansar. Mañana veremos.

—Por lo menos puedo ayudar a Elena con los quehaceres. Dime, Elena, ¿qué haces normalmente?

—Pues hago la cama, arreglo mi dormitorio, pongo la mesa. A veces voy de compras o echo una mano con la limpieza. ¿Sabes lo que menos me gusta? Pasar la aspiradora. ¿A ti te gusta?

Lo que menos me gusta es pasar la aspiradora.

—No tanto. Lo que más me gusta es guisar; sobre todo me gusta preparar los postres. Lo peor es planchar y fregar los platos. En casa tenemos turnos porque a nadie le gusta. Mi padre es quien se encarga del jardín.

Reflexive Verbs

—¿Cómo es tu casa?
—Ni grande ni pequeña. Tiene tres dormitorios, y antes tenía que compartir el mío con mi hermana mayor, pero ya se ha casado. Hay un salón, un comedor, y abajo una cocina. Arriba están los dormitorios y el cuarto de baño. Tenemos un garaje y un pequeño jardín delante de la casa y uno más grande detrás.
—¿Tu hermano también ayuda en casa?
—Sí, claro.
—Los míos, no. Tienen que estudiar mucho. Claro que mamá es ama de casa, y tu madre tiene empleo. Es distinto.

Vocabulary

peinarse to do one's hair	**pasar la aspiradora** to vacuum
la contraventana shutter	**¿a ti te gusta?** do *you* like it?
la maceta de flores pot with flowers	**no tanto** not much
	guisar to do the cooking
dar al patio to look out on to the inner courtyard	**sobre todo** especially
	preparar los postres to make puddings
el portero, la portera caretaker	
tender ropa to hang out washing	**lo peor** the worst thing
¿puedo ayudarla? can I help you?	**planchar** to iron
quitar la mesa to clear the table	**fregar los platos** to wash the dishes
por lo menos at least	
los quehaceres chores	**tener turnos** to take turns
hacer la cama to make one's bed	**a nadie le gusta** nobody likes
arreglar el dormitorio to tidy one's bedroom	**encargarse de** to take charge of
	compartir to share
poner la mesa to set the table	**abajo** downstairs
echar una mano con la limpieza to give a hand with the cleaning	**arriba** upstairs
	el ama (f) **de casa** housewife
lo que menos/más me gusta what I like least/best	**es distinto** it's different

Reflexive Verbs

These verbs indicate an action done by the person who is the subject of the verb to him/herself ('I wash myself'; 'he dresses himself'). They can also mean 'to each other', as in: *nos miramos* – 'we look at each other'.

me levanto	I get up
te despiertas	you wake up
se viste	s/he dresses, you dress

nos escondemos   we hide
os marcháis   you go away
se duermen   they go to sleep, you go to sleep

The reflexive pronoun agrees with the subject, whatever part of the verb is used. After the infinitive, the pronoun will be *se* only if the subject is 'he', 'she', 'you' or 'they'.

    e.g. *Vamos a sentarnos.*   We're going to sit down.
          Tienes que lavarte.   You've got to wash.

Other Uses of 'se'

a)   *Se* is also used impersonally, like the English 'one'.

    e.g. *¿Se puede?*   May one, is it allowed?
        (NB *¿Puedo?*   May I?)
        ¿Se puede aparcar aquí?   Is parking allowed here?

b)   *Se* is used with the third person singular or plural verb instead of the English passive (something is or was done).

    e.g. *Se habla inglés aquí*   English is spoken here
          Se venden peras   Pears for sale
          Se vende   For sale   *Se alquila*   To let

Asking Questions

1. The Simplest Way

Write a statement with a question mark, or say it in a questioning voice.

    ¿El autobús sale a las once?   The bus leaves at eleven?
    ¿Miguel vive en Plasencia?   Does Miguel live in Plasencia?
    ¿Vd. quiere más vino?   Would you like more wine?

2. Word Order

Change the word order, so that the subject follows the verb:

    ¿Sale el autobús a las once?   Does the bus leave at eleven?
    ¿Vive Miguel en Plasencia?   Does Miguel live in Plasencia?
    ¿Quiere Vd. más vino?   Would you like more wine?

• Unlike English, the subject can follow the verb when it is NOT asking a question:

Salió el tren a las diez.
El tren salió a las diez.

Both mean 'The train left at ten'.

Asking Questions

3. '¿No?' and '¿verdad?'

Add *¿no?* or *¿verdad?* to the end of your statement. This is like 'isn't it?', 'didn't they?', etc.:

El autobús sale a las once, ¿no?   The bus goes at eleven, doesn't it?
Miguel vive en Plasencia, ¿verdad?   Miguel lives in Plasencia, doesn't he?

4. Question Words

These have an accent when they ask a question, but not otherwise.
 e.g. *¿Cuándo llegó?*   When did he arrive?
But: *Cuando llegó, telefoneó a su madre.*   When he arrived, he phoned his mother.

¿cuándo? when?   *¿dónde?* where?   *¿qué?* what?
¿cómo? how? why? what? (when you haven't heard what's been said)   *¿por qué?* (two words) why?

NB *porque* (one word) = because

5. Question Words That Agree

¿quién? who? (one person)   *¿quiénes?* (more than one person)
¿cuál? which? (one only)   *¿cuáles?* (more than one item)
¿cuánto? (m. sing.), *¿cuánta?* (f. sing.), *¿cuántos?* (m. pl.), and *¿cuántas?* (f. pl.) meaning 'how much?' or 'how many?', agree with the noun which follows or which is replaced:

 e.g. *¿Tienes sellos? – Sí, ¿cuántos quieres?*   Have you any stamps? Yes, how many (agrees with *sellos*, m. pl.) do you want?

When asking a question, or after a preposition, *quien* or *quienes* must be used for people. When 'who' joins two parts of a sentence, use *que* for both people and things (who, that, which).

 e.g. *¿Quién es la chica con quien hablabas?*   Who is the girl you were talking to?
 Es la chica que trabaja en el banco.   It's the girl who works in the bank.

6. 'Qué' or 'Cuál'?

¿Qué? + *ser* asks for a definition of a thing (not a person).

 e.g. *¿Qué es esto? – Es un bolígrafo.*   What's this? It's a pen.

¿Cuál?, ¿cuáles? asks you to make a choice. It can be used for things or people:

 e.g. *¿Cuál es tu programa preferido?*   What's your favourite programme?

¿Cuáles de tus amigos van a España este año? Which of your friends are going to Spain this year?

7. Some Useful Questions

¿Para qué sirve? What is it for?   *Sirve para pelar patatas.* It's for peeling potatoes.

¿Para qué sirve?

¿De quién es? Whose is it?   *Es de Cristina.* It's Cristina's.
¿De qué es? What's it made of?   *Es de madera.* It's made of wood.
¿De qué color es? What colour is it?
¿Cómo es el nuevo profesor? What's the new teacher like?

In the Tourist Office

—¿Tiene un plano de Sevilla, por favor?
—Sí, claro. Aquí tiene. Y también hay un folleto con los lugares de interés y los monumentos que se pueden visitar. ¿Quiere una lista de hoteles? ¿O de excursiones desde Sevilla?
—No, gracias. ¿Puede indicarme en el plano dónde estoy exactamente?
—Pues mire. Aquí está el río Guadalquivir y el puente de San Telmo. A la izquierda hay la Avenida de la Constitución, con Correos, y enfrente la catedral. La oficina de turismo está aquí, a mano derecha.
—Gracias. Adiós.
—De nada, señorita. Adiós.

Vocabulary

el plano	town plan	**los lugares de interés**	places of interest
el mapa	map		
el folleto	leaflet	**el monumento nacional**	historic monument

Tourist Vocabulary

un horario de excursiones a timetable of excursions
una guía guidebook
la guía del ocio 'What's On', entertainment guide
de interés turistico interesting for tourists
una visita acompañada guided tour
un viaje organizado package tour
cerrado domingos y días festivos closed Sundays and public holidays
el día laborable working day

Asking the Way

To attract someone's attention, say *por favor* (English 'excuse me').

1. To ask for somewhere specific, 'Where is . . .?', say:

   Por favor, ¿ dónde . . . — Excuse me, where . . .
   . . . está la oficina de turismo? — . . . is the tourist office?
   . . . están los servicios? — . . . are the toilets?

2. More simply, just name what you're looking for, in a questioning voice:

   Por favor, ¿la estación de ferrocarril? — Where is the railway station, please?
   ¿El casco viejo, por favor? — Where is the old part of the town?

3. To find out if there's one nearby, 'Is there a . . . near here?', say:

   ¿Hay un centro comercial por aquí? — Is there a shopping centre near here?

4. For 'How do you get to . . . ?' 'Which is the way to . . . ?', say:

   ¿Por dónde se va . . . — Which is the way . . .
   . . . a Pamplona? — . . . to Pamplona?
   . . . al aeropuerto? — . . . to the airport?

Useful Phrases

¿está lejos? is it far?
está bastante cerca it's quite near
¿hay autobuses? are there buses?
sería mejor coger un taxi you'd better take a taxi
está . . .
  . . . a unos 15 kilometros
  . . . a más de/casi 10 kilómetros
  . . . a unos cinco minutos

¿se puede ir andando? can one walk?
¿a qué distancia está? how far is it?
¿a cuántos kilómetros está Elche? how many kilometres is it to Elche?
it's . . .
  . . . about 15 kilometres
  . . . more than/almost 10 kilometres
  . . . about five minutes away

Giving Directions

1. Use the present tense.
   Vd. sigue todo recto, luego cruce la Plaza Mayor y coge la calle que sale a la derecha.
   You go straight on, then you cross the Plaza Mayor and you take the street going to the right.
2. Use the polite imperative for strangers, the familiar imperative for friends.

Vd. (polite)	*tú* (familiar)	
siga todo recto	*sigue todo recto*	go straight on
tome	*toma*	take
coja	*coge*	take
tuerza	*tuerce*	turn
cruce	*cruza*	cross
baje	*baja*	go down
suba	*sube*	go up

3. Use *tener que* + infinitive; or *hay que* + infinitive.
   Tener will agree with the subject (*tú tienes*, *Vd. tiene*) but *hay* does not change.
   e.g. *Tienes que (Hay que) bajar hasta los semáforos, luego atrevesar el puente.*
   You have to go down as far as the traffic-lights, then cross the bridge.
4. In written instructions the infinitive may be used, especially in recipes or manuals.
   e.g. *Dirigirse a la portería.*   Apply to the caretaker.

Vocabulary for Directions

siga las indicaciones follow the signs	**el paso de peatones** pedestrian crossing
al final de la calle at the end of the street	**pulse el botón** press the button
	espere wait
la primera bocacalle a la derecha the first street/turning on the right	**el paso a nivel** level crossing
	la cuesta hill (in town)
	la autopista motorway
la cuarta calle a la izquierda the fourth street on the left	**el peaje** motorway tollbooth
	la carretera road between towns
a mano derecha on the right	**la autovía** dual carriageway

'Ser' or 'Estar'?

Both mean 'to be', but they are used in different situations.

ser	estar
1. To say what something is: *Madrid es la capital de España.* Madrid is the capital of Spain. 2. For unchanging conditions: *Pedro es muy alegre.* Pedro's a very cheerful person. 3. For the date: —*¿Qué fecha es hoy?* —*Es el treinta de agosto.* What date is it today? It's the 30th of August. 4. For nationality: *Son españoles.* They're Spanish. —*¿De dónde eres?* —*Soy de Valencia.* Where are you from? I'm from Valencia. 5. For people's jobs: *Su marido es ingeniero.* Her husband's an engineer. 6. For colour: *La puerta es amarilla.* The door is yellow. 7. For ownership: —*¿Estas tijeras son tuyas?* —*No, son de Blanca.* Are these scissors yours? No, they're Blanca's. 8. For what things are made of: *La blusa es de seda.* The blouse is made of silk.	1. To say where something is: *Madrid está en el centro de España.* Madrid is in the centre of Spain. 2. For temporary states: *La tienda está cerrada.* The shop is closed. *Pedro está triste hoy.* Pedro's unhappy today. 3. For the date: —*¿A cuántos estamos hoy?* —*Estamos a seis de enero.* What date is it today? It's the 6th of January. 4. For health: *¿Estás enfermo?* Are you ill? 5. In continuous tenses: *Estamos estudiando el italiano.* We're learning Italian. *Estaban durmiendo.* They were sleeping.

- Some adjectives have different meanings with *ser* or *estar*.
  Jaime es muy listo. Jaime is very clever.
  But: *Jaime está listo.* Jaime's ready.
  And: *El niño es muy malo.* The child's very naughty.
  Soy muy malo en física. I'm very bad at physics.
  But: *El niño está muy malo.* The child is very ill.

Describing Where You Live

Make sure you can describe your town and the district you live in, and if you've been to Spain, the places you visited and your reactions to them. Include:
  where it is – north, south, near London
  what kind of place it is – size, industries, tourist attractions
  the surroundings – sea, hills, river
  places of interest – castle, museums, sports stadium, university
  entertainments – cinemas, discos, fishing, ice-skating
  whether you like it, why, and where you'd prefer to live

Vocabulary

vivo a orillas del mar I live at the seaside	**en un pueblo de pescadores** in a fishing village
en las afueras de Liverpool in the outskirts of Liverpool	**el ayuntamiento** the town hall
	el alcalde mayor
en un barrio nuevo in a new district	**el parque de atracciones** amusement park
cerca del estadio near the stadium	**aislado, -da** isolated

Examples

a) Newtown es una ciudad moderna con mucha industria. Fabrican productos químicos. Alrededor hay muchas minas de carbón. Newtown es muy feo y sucio, con mucho tráfico, y a veces huele mal, pero a mí me gusta vivir allí porque hay mucho que hacer y hay una cantidad de discotecas y bares, tres cines y un teatro, varios centros polideportivos, y el mejor equipo de fútbol de toda Inglaterra.

b) Oldcastle es una ciudad muy pintoresca e histórica. Se puede visitar el castillo, la catedral, el museo y las murallas. Hay ruinas romanas, una torre medieval, un monastrio en ruinas, y un río donde se puede alquilar un barco de remos. Pero no todo es antiguo. Muchos turistas extranjeros llegan para la fiesta de música en el verano, y por eso hay muchos hoteles, muy buenas tiendas y una gran variedad de restaurantes. Creo que tengo mucha suerte de poder vivir en una ciudad tan agradable.

Useful Words and Phrases
Which Is Best?

antes vivíamos en el norte, cerca de Leeds	we used to live in the north, near Leeds
nos trasladamos aquí hace dos años	we moved here two years ago
al principio no me gustó	at first I didn't like it
una ventaja de vivir aquí es que...	one advantage of living here is that...
el único inconveniente de mi barrio es que...	the only disadvantage of my part of town is that...
una pandilla de amigos	a gang of friends
prefiero el campo porque...	I prefer the country because...
...es más tranquilo	...it's quieter
...hay menos ruido	...there's less noise
...es más limpio	...it's cleaner
...todo el mundo se conoce	...everybody knows everyone else
no me gusta vivir en el campo porque...	I don't like living in the country because...
...es aburrido	...it's boring
...no hay nada que hacer	...there's nothing to do
...no puedo salir de noche	...I can't go out at night
prefiero la ciudad porque...	I prefer the town because...
...es más animada	...it's more lively
...hay más distracciones	...there's more to do
si podía escoger, me gustaría vivir en California	if I could choose, I'd like to live in California

Spain is Different

en España...	in Spain...
...comen a las tres y cenan a las diez	...they have lunch at three and supper at ten
...la gente es más abierta, más cariñosa, pero hacen mucho ruido y se abrazan con frecuencia	...people are more open, more warm, but very noisy and they hug each other all the time
...el clima es distinto, hace más sol y más calor y llueve menos	...the climate's different: it's sunnier and hotter and rains less

Think of others for yourself.

The Reading Test

You will not understand every word, since genuine notices, advertisements, leaflets, etc. will be used. What you have to do is extract information, or explain what the item is about.

1. <u>Make sense.</u> What you say must mean something to an English-speaking person. For instance, on the back of a bus you see the following notice. What does it ask you to do?

> *Permítame salir*

Think what you would see on an English bus. The answer is not 'Permit me to leave' (which is a translation), but 'Let buses pull out'.

2. <u>Read to the end.</u> Always read the whole question. Don't stop when you think you've found the answer. This notice is pinned to the door of a castle. When is it open in summer?

> *Abierto todos los días de 9.30 a 13.30, incluso días festivos. En invierno cerrado domingos y días festivos. Cerrado en agosto.*

You read to *en invierno*, and may think the answer is 'every day from 9.30 a.m. to 1.30 p.m.' But after the winter closing-times comes *cerrado en agosto*. The correct answer must include 'closed all August'.

3. <u>Include all relevant details.</u> Always re-read the question after writing your answer to make sure you haven't left out anything which could be relevant. For example, the question reads:

This notice is on the door of the supermarket.

> *Aviso*
> *Todos los domingos desde el 30 de septiembre cerraremos a las 12.30.*

What will happen from 30 September?
'It will close at 12.30' is not enough – you <u>must</u> include 'on Sundays'.

Vocabulary for Common Signs

consigna left luggage
ojo al tren beware of trains
aseos toilets
particular private
no funciona out of order
en el acto while you wait
obras roadworks
desvío diversion
peligroso adelantar dangerous to overtake
puerto cerrado pass (in mountains) closed
prohibido el paso no entry
ceder el paso give way

avisamos grúa parked cars will be towed away
limitación de velocidad speed limit
mantenga limpia la ciudad keep the town clean
no tire colillas don't throw cigarette ends
descanso theatre or cinema closed for the day
no pisar el césped keep off the grass
sólo turismos private cars only

Listening Practice

1. Using the plan of Logroño below, follow the instructions given to you by a passer-by to get to the railway station. You're standing outside the Tourist Office (No. 10 on plan), facing the park. Where is the station?

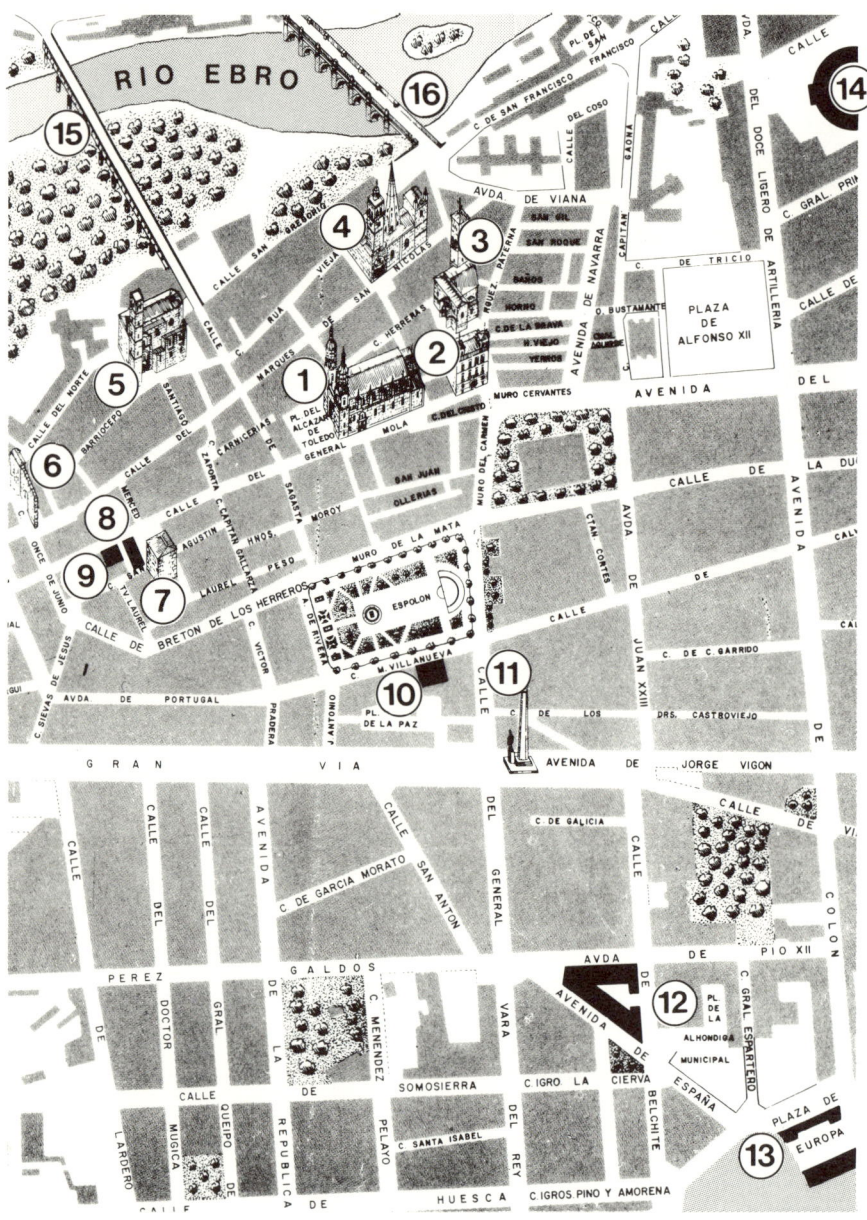

Listening Practice

2. (Higher level) You've arranged to meet a friend at a hotel in Logroño, but you can't find it. You go into the Tourist Office and ask them for directions. Put your finger on the Tourist Office (No. 10 on plan) and follow the route as you hear it. Where is the hotel?

3. Listen carefully to Javier's father reading it aloud, and decide which of the three postcards below Javier sent home from holiday.

Speaking Practice

Answers:
1. In the Plaza de Europa
2. In the Plaza de San Francisco
3. Tossa (the only one with a castle)

Speaking Practice

1. You have just arrived to stay with your Spanish pen-friend for the first time. He's explaining the daily routine to you:
    Here's your room. The bathroom's opposite.
    a) Say you like it – it's a nice room.
    We usually have breakfast in the kitchen.
    b) Ask what time he gets up in the morning.
    About 7.30. What do you have for breakfast?
    c) Tell him tea or coffee with toast and butter.
    Don't you have eggs at home?
    d) Say no, but sometimes you have orange juice.
2. (Higher level) Someone stops you in the street and asks:
    Is there a bank near here?
    a) Say there is, but it's closed after 2 p.m.
    Do you know where I can change a traveller's cheque?
    b) Tell her the airport has a 'cambio'.
    How can I get there?
    c) Tell her to catch the number 37 bus in front of the station.
    Is it far?
    d) Tell her it's half an hour away by bus.

3 Planning a Party

This chapter deals with giving invitations, accepting and refusing them; asking permission; apologising; talking about your free time, sports and hobbies (including bullfights!); likes and dislikes; introducing people; and how to translate 'to meet'. The grammar section revises the time, dates and numbers; negative expressions; the continuous present tense and the gerund (present participle).

Elena Plans a Party

—¿Qué haces el sábado en Inglaterra, Sarah?

—Por lo general, salgo con amigos, vamos al cine o a una discoteca, o a casa de un amigo a escuchar discos o charlar. Dos veces mis padres me dejaron ir a un concierto de música pop, cuando mi conjunto favorito tocaba en Bradford, pero tuve que ir con mis primos mayores; no me permiten ir sola. ¿Y tú?

—Igual que tú, o salgo con mis padres a cenar. Oye, ¿qué te parece si invito a mis amigos a casa mañana, para conocerte? Podemos ofrecerles refrescos y algo de comer.

—A mí me parece estupendo. Pero ¿qué dirán tus padres?

—Nada, si yo lo preparo todo y limpio la casa después. ¿Tienes cassettes de cantantes ingleses?

—Unos pocos. Te puedo preparar unos 'perritos calientes', si quieres.

—¡Genial! Vamos a tener una fiesta inglesa, con patatas fritas, cocacola, hamburguesas y salchichas. Y tarta de manzana. ¿Te parece bien? Voy a pedir permiso a mis padres, luego invitaré a todo el mundo.

• • • • •

—Dígame.

—Oye, ¿eres Juana? Vamos a tener una pequeña fiesta mañana por la tarde. ¿Estás libre? Quiero presentar a Sarah a todos mis amigos.

—Sí, mañana no hago nada. Me encantaría ir. ¿A qué hora?

—Alrededor de las ocho. Y otra cosa, ¿quieres traer unos discos?

—Por supuesto. Hasta mañana, entonces.

• • • • •

—¿Está Ramón?

—Soy yo. ¿Quién es?

—Hola Ramón. Soy Elena. ¿Te gustaría venir a casa mañana por la tarde, a conocer a mi amiga inglesa?

—¿Mañana? ¡Qué pena! Lo siento mucho, pero mañana no puedo. Es el santo de mi madre.

Vocabulary

por lo general generally	el cantante singer
charlar to chat	el perrito caliente hot dog
me dejaron ir they let me go, they allowed me to go	¡genial! terrific, brilliant
	la salchicha sausage
no me permiten ir sola they don't let me go alone	pedir permiso to ask permission
	una fiesta party (also holiday)
igual que tú same as you	alrededor de about
¿qué te parece? what do you think?	por supuesto of course
	¿está Ramón? is Ramón in?
el refresco soft drink	qué pena what a shame
¿qué dirán tus padres? what will your parents say?	el santo name day (celebrated like birthday)

Useful Words and Phrases

Asking Permission

¿puedo salir? may I go out?
¿es posible ducharme? is it possible to have a shower?
quisiera visitar Ronda I'd like to visit Ronda
¿sería posible telefonear a mis padres? would it be possible to phone my parents?
con permiso excuse me, allow me

Vd.	tú		
¿me deja ¿me permite	¿me dejas ¿me permites	abrir la ventana?	will you let me open the window?
¿le molesta si ¿le importa si	¿te molesta si ¿te importa si	abro la ventana?	do you mind if I open the window?

Forbidding

está prohibido aparcar en la acera it's forbidden to park on the pavement
se prohíbe entrar no entry
prohibido fumar no smoking
¡perros no! no dogs
se ruega no hacer ruido you are asked not to make a noise
no se admiten menores no admittance under 18

Requests

Informal:
¿quieres comprarme una revista? will you buy me a magazine?
por favor, ¿puedes echarme una mano? can you give me a hand?
¿me haces el favor de echar esta carta al buzón? will you be very kind and post this letter?

Useful Words and Phrases

More formal:
hágame el favor de comprobar el aceite kindly check the oil
tenga la bondad de subir esta maleta would you be good enough to take this suitcase up

se ruega apagar la luz please turn off the light
sírvase Vd. cerrar la puerta con llave please lock your door
(The above two examples are for written notices)

Invitations

¿te apetece tomar un café? do you feel like a coffee?
¿por qué no vamos al cine? why don't we go to the cinema?
¿tienes ganas de ir a la playa? do you fancy going to the beach?
¿jugamos al tenis? shall we play tennis?
¿te gustaría . . .
 . . . pasar el verano en Algeciras?
 . . . pasar el día conmigo?
 . . . venir a casa?

vamos a tomar una copita/un helado let's go and have a drink/an ice-cream
si estás en Fuengirola, no te olvides de venir a vernos if you're in Fuengirola, be sure to come and see us

would you like to . . .
 . . . spend the summer in Algeciras?
 . . . spend the day with me?
 . . . come to my house?

Accepting

me encantaría I'd love to
sí, con mucho gusto yes, with pleasure
gracias, es Vd. muy amable thank you, you're very kind

de acuerdo ⎱ agreed, fine,
vale ⎰ OK, right
¡qué buena idea! what a good idea!

Refusing

lo siento mucho, pero no puedo aceptar I'm very sorry I can't accept
¡qué lástima! estoy citado, -da what a pity. I've got an engagement, a date
tengo una cita con Isabel I've got a date with Isabel
siento mucho no poder acompañarte I'm very sorry I can't go with you
me encantaría, pero tengo la gripe I'd love to, but I've got 'flu

no me apetece nada I don't feel like it at all
no tengo ganas I don't fancy it
lamento no poder aceptar la invitación I regret I am unable to accept the invitation
no me interesa el fútbol en absoluto I'm not a bit interested in football
me aburren las películas de miedo Horror films bore me
estoy ocupado, -da hoy I'm busy today

33

Apologising

¡Vd. disculpe! } sorry!
¡perdóneme! }
discúlpeme por haberle molestado
   forgive me for having disturbed you
¿le molesto? am I disturbing you?
por desgracia . . .
   unfortunately . . .
   . . . se me cayó
     . . . I dropped it
   . . . el gato lo comió
     . . . the cat ate it
   . . . se me olvidó . . . I forgot
haré todo lo posible para . . . I'll do my best to . . .
siento lo que ocurrió I'm sorry for what happened
siento mucho contestarte tan tarde I'm very sorry I'm replying so late

admito que me equivoqué I admit I was mistaken/wrong
la culpa es mía it's my fault
fue sin querer I didn't mean to do it
lo hice sin pensar I didn't think

¿Le molesto?

lamentamos tener que decirle que . . . we regret to tell you that . . .

Replying to Apologies

no hay de que don't mention it
no es nada it's nothing
es igual it doesn't matter
no importa (en absoluto)
   it doesn't matter (in the slightest)

no tiene importancia it's not important
no lo pienses más think no more about it
no te preocupes don't worry

Arranging to Meet

iré a buscarte a tu casa I'll pick you up at your house
¿dónde nos vemos? }
¿dónde nos veremos? } where shall we meet?
¿cómo quedamos? }

¿a qué hora quedamos? what time shall we meet?
nos encontramos en el Bar Velázquez we'll meet in the Velazquez Bar
nos veremos delante del cine we'll meet outside the cinema

Introducing People

¿conoces a Yolanda? do you know Yolanda?
sí, nos conocimos ayer en casa de Rocío yes, we met yesterday at Rocío's

encantado (if you are male) . . .
encantada (if you are female) . . .
   . . . how do you do?
mucho gusto (conocerle/la) pleased to meet you

> **le presento a mi padre** (formal) } this is my father/let me introduce
> **te presento a mi padre** (to a friend) } you to my father

Negative Words

Most negative words can be placed before or after the verb. Before the verb they are stronger: *no fuma nunca* simply states a fact, 'he never smokes'; *nunca fuma* stresses the 'never', 'he never smokes'. When the negative word comes AFTER the verb, *no* must be placed before the verb.

no miento { *nunca* / *jamás* }	{ *nunca* / *jamás* } *miento*	I never lie
no ve nada	*nada ve*	he sees nothing, he doesn't see anything
no viene nadie	*nadie viene*	nobody's coming
¿no conoces a nadie?	*¿a nadie conoces?*	don't you know anyone? (personal *a* because *nadie* is a person and the object of *conoces*)
no sabemos nadar tampoco	*tampoco sabemos nadar*	we can't swim either
no queda ningún periódico	*ningún periódico queda*	not a newspaper is left
no queda ninguno	*ninguno queda*	not one is left

ni siquiera me mira   he doesn't even look at me

ni saben ni quieren saber   they neither know nor want to know

ya no   not any longer, no more

patinaba antes, pero ya no   I used to skate, but not any more

para siempre jamás   for ever and ever

nunca jamás   never ever

- In English a double negative is not correct. We don't say 'he doesn't never speak to nobody' but 'he doesn't ever speak to anybody'. In Spanish, whenever a phrase begins with a negative word (including *sin*, 'without'), everything that follows must be negative.
  e.g. *No ve nunca a nadie.*   He never sees anybody.
  Sin pagar nunca nada   Without ever paying anything

Seasons, Dates and Numbers
Seasons

la estación del año season of the year	**los veraneantes** summer holiday-makers
la temporada season (plays, films)	**estival** (adjective) summer
temporada alta/baja high/low season	

Dates

De is needed before the month and year:
Es el dos de junio de 1991.
At the top of letters, *el* is left out but *de* is still needed:
30 de septiembre de 1991
To say a date out loud, begin with a thousand, then hundreds, then tens and units (NOT 'nineteen forty nine' but 'one thousand, nine hundred, forty and nine').
   e.g. *1066   mil sesenta y seis   2000   dos mil*

Numbers

a) *Y* is only used between tens and units. Thus 910 is *novecientos diez*, NOT *y diez*; and 101 is *ciento uno*, without *y* because there are no tens; but 537 is *quinientos treinta y siete*.

b) Hundreds are formed as in English, but written as one word: 300 is *trescientos*, and 400 is *cuatrocientos*. There are three irregular hundreds:
   500 *quinientos*   700 *setecientos*   900 *novecientos*

c) Before a feminine noun like *pesetas*, numbers from 200 to 900 agree.
   e.g. *seiscientas pesetas*   six hundred pesetas

d) One hundred has no 'one' in Spanish and is *cien* before a noun.
   e.g. *cien veces*   a hundred times
   cien pesetas   a hundred pesetas
   Before a number it is *ciento*.
   e.g. *ciento cincuenta*.

e) When a number ends in *-uno* it loses the *-o* before a masculine noun, and becomes *-una* before a feminine noun.
   e.g. *veintiuno*   twenty-one
   But: *veintiún años, ciento un meses*   twenty-one years, one hundred and one months
   sesenta y una horas   sixty-one hours

The Time

Until half-past the hour, add *y* and the number of minutes. After half-past, take the next hour and subtract the minutes.

Basic Vocabulary

¿tienes hora? can you tell me the time?
es/era la una it is/was one o'clock
son/eran las dos it is/was two o'clock

da/daba la una it is/was striking one
daban/dieron las doce it was striking/struck twelve

¿Qué hora es?	What time is it?
Son las cuatro y cuarto	It's a quarter past four
y diez	ten past
y media	half past
menos cuarto	quarter to
menos veinticinco	twenty-five to
Son las seis en punto	It's exactly six o'clock
y pico	just after six

¿A qué hora?	At what time?
A las siete de la tarde	At 7 p.m.
A las ocho de la mañana	At 8 a.m.
A las once de la noche	At 11 p.m.
A las tres de la madrugada	At 3 a.m.
Alrededor de las nueve	Around nine

- *La tarde* begins at noon and is used until dark or after 10 p.m. It then becomes *la noche*.

Useful Expressions

mañana por la mañana tomorrow morning
ayer por la tarde yesterday afternoon/evening
pasado mañana the day after tomorrow
anoche last night
anteayer the day before yesterday
la noche anterior the night before
la semana/el año que viene next week/year
domingo pasado last Sunday

el martes on Tuesday (no word for 'on')
los martes on Tuesdays
a la hora de comer at lunch time
a primera hora first thing
a última hora at the last minute
perder tiempo to waste time
sin perder tiempo without delay
al mismo tiempo at the same time
a poco tiempo soon after
llegar a tiempo to arrive in time
la próxima vez next time

'For' with Time

1. Leave out 'for'.
    Estuvimos allí tres días.   We were there for three days.
    Vivió cinco años en Ecuador.   He lived in Ecuador for five years.
2. Use *durante*.
    Llovió durante media hora.   It rained for half an hour.
3. Use *por* (but never *para*) for previously planned length of time.
    Voy a Méjico por un mes.   I'm going to Mexico for a month.
4. To say 'I have been doing something for . . .' (and you still are), use the present tense or the *continuous present tense. (English uses perfect tense.)

    a) *Hace* + time + *que* + present tense
           Hace dos años que estudio el español.
    b) Continuous present + *desde hace* + time
           Estoy estudiando el español desde hace dos años.
    c) Present tense of *llevar* + time + gerund
           Llevo dos años estudiando el español.

    I've been studying Spanish for two years.

5. To say 'How long have you been . . . ?', use the following.
    ¿Desde cuándo aprendes el español?
    ¿Cuánto tiempo hace que aprendes el español?
    ¿Cuánto tiempo llevas aprendiendo el español?

    How long have you been learning Spanish?

6. For time further back in the past (How long HAD you been . . . ?), change *hace* to *hacía* and use the imperfect or continuous imperfect tense.
    Hacía dos años que estudiaba el español cuando . . .
    Estudiaba el español desde hacía dos años cuando . . .
    Llevaba dos años estudiando el espanol cuando . . .
    I had been studying Spanish for two years when . . .
    ● Use PRESENT if you still ARE, and IMPERFECT if you still WERE.
7. *Hace* + time means 'ago'.
    Aprendí el español hace dos años.   I learnt Spanish two years ago. (and am not learning now).

*see next section

The Continuous Present

Spanish, like English, has a continuous present tense as well as the present tense (see Chapter 1). It is used to emphasise what you are actually doing now.

The Continuous Present

Present	Continuous Present
¿*Qué haces por la tarde?* What do you do in the evening?	¿*Qué estás haciendo ahora?* What are you doing now?
Veo la televisión. I watch television.	*Estoy viendo la televisión.* I'm watching television.
Juego mucho al fútbol. I play a lot of football.	*Estoy jugando al fútbol.* I'm playing football (now).

Formation of Gerund and Continuous Present

The continuous present is formed from the present tense of *estar* + gerund (present participle). To make the gerund, remove the last two letters from the infinitive and add *-ando* for *-ar* verbs, *-iendo* for *-er* and *-ir* verbs.

    llamar   remove *-ar*,   add *-ando*,   *llamando*   calling
    comer   remove *-er*,   add *-iendo*,   *comiendo*   eating
    salir   remove *-ir*,   add *-iendo*,   *saliendo*   leaving

Radical changing verbs in *-ir* change o→u, or e→i.
    e.g. *dormir*   *durmiendo*,   sleeping
        pedir   *pidiendo*,   asking for

● The gerund never agrees and always ends in *-o*:

estoy hablando	I am talking
estás aprendiendo	you are learning
está viviendo	s/he, you(*Vd.*) is/are living
estamos buscando	we are looking for
estáis haciendo	you are making
están escribiendo	they, you(*Vds.*) are writing

Unusual Gerunds

decir	*diciendo*,	speaking		*leer*	*leyendo*,	reading
venir	*viniendo*,	coming		*oír*	*oyendo*,	hearing
caer	*cayendo*,	falling		*traer*	*trayendo*,	bringing

Use

a) *Tener*, *ser*, *estar* and *ir* are not normally used in the continuous present; use the present tense instead.

b) The gerund can be used on its own, so long as it is used as a verb and not an adjective.
    e.g. *Leyendo el periódico, mi padre vio este anuncio.*
        Reading the newspaper, my father saw this advertisement.
        Los niños aprenden mucho jugando.
        Children learn a lot (by) playing.

But: *Su mujer es encantadora.* His wife is charming.
Mi hermana tiene un loro que habla. My sister has a talking parrot. (because 'charming' and 'talking' are adjectives, describing 'wife' and 'parrot')

To Meet

There are a number of words in Spanish for 'to meet'.
1. *Conocer*, to meet for the first time, to get to know:
   Nos conocimos en Gibraltar el verano pasado.
   We met in Gibraltar last summer.

2. *Encontrar*, to meet someone you already know:
   Encontraron a Dolores en el café.
   They met Dolores in the café.

3. *Encontrarse con, dar con*, to meet by chance:
   Dimos con tu antiguo profesor en Menorca.
   We ran into your old teacher in Minorca.

4. *Quedar (en)*, to arrange to meet:
   ¿Dónde quedamos entonces?
   Where shall we meet then?
   Quedamos en encontrarnos a las seis.
   We arranged to meet at six.

5. *Reunirse con*, to meet, get together, have a meeting:
   Nos reunimos todos los años en Marbella.
   We meet up every year in Marbella.
   La junta se reúne cada mes.
   The committee meets every month.

Nos reunimos todos los años en Marbella.

Free Time

¿Qué te gusta hacer en tus ratos libres? What do you like to do in your free time?

a) Games, **jugar a**
      juego al ajedrez   I play chess
      jugaba al volante   I used to play badminton
      jugué a los dardos   I played darts
b) Music, **tocar**
      toco la flauta   I play the flute
      tocaba el violoncelo   I used to play the cello
      toqué la batería   I played the drums

c) **hago mucho deporte**   I do a lot of sport
    hacía atletismo   I used to do athletics
    hice gimnasia   I did gymnastics
d) **practico el esquí acuático**   I water ski
    practicaba el remo   I used to row
    practiqué el boxeo   I boxed
e) **me entusiasma el baile**   I love dancing
        la vela   sailing
        la pesca   fishing

Me encanta hacer punto.

f) **me interesa la costura**   I'm interested in sewing
        construir maquetas   making models
        coleccionar sellos   stamp collecting
g) **me encanta hacer punto**   I love knitting
        la lectura   reading
        leer novelas policiacas   reading detective novels
        leer tebeos   reading comics
h) **me gusta ir de paseo**   I like going for walks
        dar un paseo en barco   going out in a boat
        dar un paseo en bicicleta   going for cycle rides
i) **pertenezco al club de judo**   I belong to the judo club
    soy entusiasta de la equitación   I'm keen on riding
    soy aficionado a la lucha   I'm a wrestling fan

Leisure Vocabulary

la cadena	TV channel	**en color**	in colour
los anuncios	advertisements	**en blanco y negro**	in black and white
las actualidades	current affairs		
la pantalla	screen	**el estreno**	first performance
los dibujos animados	cartoons	**la sesión de tarde**	afternoon performance
la serie	soap opera		
el conjunto	group	**la sesión continua**	continuous showing
la gira	tour		
el elepé	long-playing record	**no apto para menores**	unsuitable for under 18
interpretar	to perform		
el descanso	interval	**la fila**	row
el acomodador, la acomodadora	usher(ette)	**la película** { **del Oeste** Western / **de espionaje** spy film }	
¿qué ponen en el Rex?	What's on at the Rex?		

Bullfights

You don't have to go to a bullfight, but you must know a bit about what happens in one and be able to explain your feelings about them.

Listening Practice

Vocabulary

ir a los toros	go to a bullfight	**el peón**	member of team
la corrida (de toros)	bullfight	**el tendido de sol**	seats in sun (cheapest)
la plaza de toros	bullring		
el torero / **el matador**	bullfighter	**... de sol y sombra**	... in the sun at first
el picador	horseman who jabs the bull with a pike	**... de sombra**	... in the shade (most expensive)
las banderillas	pairs of long darts put into bull's neck		
la cuadrilla	bullfighter's team		

Arguments For and Against Bullfighting

FOR	AGAINST
Se llama 'el deporte nacional de España'. It's called Spain's national sport.	*No es un deporte, es una matanza/un asesinato.* It's not a sport, it's slaughter/murder.
Es algo tradicional y muy típico. It's something traditional and very typical.	*Es muy cruel.* It's very cruel.
Es un espectáculo artístico como el ballet. It's artistic, like ballet.	*No puedo ver la sangre.* I can't bear the blood.
El matador debe mostrar mucho valor y habilidad. The bullfighter must show a lot of courage and skill.	*El toro no gana nunca.* The bull never wins.
Quiero verlo antes de decidirme. I want to see it before I make up my mind.	*Me molesta ver a un hombre matar a un animal.* It upsets me to watch a man kill an animal.
No se debe criticar lo que no se ha visto nunca. You shouldn't criticise what you've never seen.	*Es sólo una manera de torturar al toro.* It's just a way of torturing the bull.

Listening Practice

1. While you are on holiday, a car with a loudspeaker tours the town advertising a new attraction.

a) What is it advertising?
  b) When will it open?
  c) What is the special offer?

2. (Higher level) Listen to this interview with a retired footballer talking about the game today.
  a) What view does he disagree with?
  b) What does he say footballers believe they are?
  c) Name two things players did not do in his day.
  d) What does he say footballers are like, and why?
  e) In his opinion, what is the only thing they're interested in?

Answers:
1. (a) A new disco (b) Tonight at eight (c) Girls will get a free bottle of perfume.
2. (a) The fans are to blame (for everything) (b) Showbiz stars (c) Wear earrings/have long hair/fight during matches (d) (Little) girls; they fall down if anyone touches them (e) Their image.

Speaking Practice

1. You go to the ticket office to buy two seats for tonight's performance. You begin:
  a) Ask for two seats in the stalls.
     I'm sorry, there are none left.
  b) Ask if she has any for tomorrow afternoon.
     Yes, how many would you like?
  c) Say two, and ask what time the performance ends.
     About 8.30.
  d) Ask if she can change a 5000 peseta note.

2. (Higher level) You are discussing with your Spanish friend where to go this evening. You begin:
  a) Invite him to see the new film at the Rex with you.
     No, I've seen it before, in Madrid.
  b) Ask him what he'd like to do.
     Why don't we go to the bullfight?
  c) Refuse, giving the reason why you don't want to go.
     He suggests you go to the new Sports Centre.
  d) Agree, and suggest you meet in the bar at 7 p.m.

4 Talking About the Future

This chapter shows you how to talk about your future plans, your school, and jobs. There is an example of a formal letter, and how to write an application for a job. The chapter gives different ways of saying you like or dislike something, and of showing approval, disapproval and surprise. The grammar section revises the future tense and tells you how to avoid the subjunctive, and there is advice on tackling the listening test.

What Do You Want to Be?

—¿Qué quieres hacer después de terminar tus estudios, Elena?

—Realmente no lo sé. Pero me gustaría viajar mucho, y tener un empleo que me interese. El dinero no me importa tanto.

—Pues a mí, sí. El sueldo es lo más importante. Quisiera ser millonario antes de los tréinta. Luego pasaría la vida divirtiéndome, con mi casa en el Caribe, el yate, los caballos de carreras, el avión particular...

—¡Imbécil! Estamos hablando en serio.

—Sarah, ¿qué quieres ser? Enfermera, secretaria, azafata, estrella de cine, novelista famosa, primera ministra...

—Por favor, José Luis. No seas tonto.

—Bueno, tengo la intención de hacerme abogado, pero de los que actúan en los procesos criminales. Me encantaría levantarme en los tribunales y atacar a los asesinos, a los atracadores, a los terroristas. Pero tendré que estudiar muchos años. ¿Y tú, Pili?

Quiero casarme y tener muchos hijos.

—Quiero casarme y ser ama de casa y tener muchos hijos. Saldré de compras, leeré revistas femeninas, jugaré al golf con mi marido, que tendrá que ser muy rico, claro.

—Yo sueño con trabajar en la tele como locutora. O si no, como periodista. Sí, seré 'nuestro enviado especial en París'. ¿Qué os parece?

Bueno, supongo que en realidad la mayoría de entre nosotros terminará trabajando en una empresa, en un banco o en una oficina.
—Yo no. No podría aguantar una oficina. Prefiero trabajar al aire libre. Voy a hacerme ingeniero agrónomo, y trabajar en el cortijo de mi abuelo.
—Y yo voy a ponerme un bar o una discoteca. Así puedo pasar la vida divirtiéndome, igual que José Luis.
—¿Nadie quiere ser profesor?
—¡Ni hablar!

Vocabulary

un empleo que me interese a job that interests me
el dinero no me importa tanto the money doesn't matter to me so much
a mí sí it does to me
el sueldo es lo más importante the salary is the most important thing
antes de los treinta before I'm thirty
el Caribe the Caribbean
el yate yacht
los caballos de carreras racehorses
el avión particular private plane
hablar en serio to talk seriously
el enfermero, la enfermera nurse
la azafata air hostess
el abogado lawyer
de los que actúan en los procesos criminales the kind who act in criminal cases

los tribunales courts
el atracador bank robber
la revista femenina women's magazine
sueño con trabajar en la tele I dream of working in television
el locutor, la locutora TV announcer
el periodista journalist
nuestro enviado especial our special correspondent
una empresa a firm
no podría aguantar una oficina I couldn't stand an office
el ingeniero agrónomo agricultural expert
el cortijo farm (in Andalusia)
poner un bar to open a bar
pasar la vida divirtiéndome to spend my life enjoying myself
igual que José Luis like José Luis
¡ni hablar! no way!

Other Useful Vocabulary

¿vas a cursar estudios superiores? are you going on to higher education?
¿en qué quieres trabajar? what do you want to work at?
me quedaré en el colegio dos años más I'll stay two more years at this (independent) school
el salario wage

pienso montar un negocio I intend to set up a business
necesito ganarme la vida I need to earn my living
hay mucho paro there's a lot of unemployment
quiero un trabajo con responsabilidad I want a job with responsibility

The Future Tense

quiero hacerme . . .	I want to become . . .
. . . investigador	. . . a research worker
. . . músico	. . . a musician
. . . político	. . . a politician

Espero ser peluquero.   *Quiero hacerme músico.*

espero ser . . .	I hope to be . . .
. . . bombero	. . . a fireman
. . . maestro, -tra	. . . a primary school teacher
. . . contable	. . . an accountant
. . . peluquero, -ra	. . . a hairdresser
quiero trabajar . . .	I want to work . . .
. . . de aprendiz	. . . as an apprentice
. . . en una agencia de viajes	. . . in a travel agency
. . . en el mundo del espectáculo	. . . in show business
. . . en la construcción	. . . in the building industry
. . . en la industria química	. . . in the chemical industry
. . . con los ordenadores	. . . with computers
quiero ser . . .	I want to be . . .
. . . funcionario, -ria	. . . a civil servant
. . . asistenta social	. . . a social worker

The Future Tense

1. 'Ir a' + Infinitive

To say what you <u>are going to do</u>, use *ir a* + infinitive.
Vamos a pasar las vacaciones en Torremolinos.   We're going to spend our holiday in Torremolinos.

2. The Future Tense

The whole of the infinitive + future endings are used to form the future tense.

hablar*é*	I shall speak
comer*ás*	you will eat
vivir*á*	s/he, you(*Vd.*) will live
comprar*emos*	we shall buy
vender*éis*	you will sell
escribir*án*	they, you(*Vds.*) will write

● The future of *hay* is *habrá*, 'there will be'.

3. Some Irregular Futures

decir	diré	I shall say	saber	sabré	I shall know
hacer	haré	do, make	salir	saldré	leave
poder	podré	be able to	tener	tendré	have
poner	pondré	put	venir	vendré	come
querer	querré	want			

4. 'Will You' Meaning 'Please' '

If the Head says 'Will you come to my room after break', he's not asking about your future plans but is telling you to do something. Spanish uses *quiere(s)* + infinitive.

e.g. *¿Quiere Vd. prestarme un lápiz?* Will you lend me a pencil, please?

5. 'Shall I?' as an Offer to Help

Questions like 'Shall I set the table?', meaning NOW, use the present tense in Spanish.

e.g. *¿Pongo la mesa?* Shall I set the table?
¿Saco las entradas? Shall I buy the tickets (now)?

Talking About School

—Hoy vas a acompañarme al Instituto, Sarah.

—¿Pero no estás de vacaciones?

—¡Qué va! El curso empieza a fines de septiembre; tenemos unos días para Navidades, y luego la Semana Santa, y el curso termina en junio. Y algunas fiestas aisladas. Semana Santa no empieza hasta la semana que viene, así que esta semana tengo clases.

—¿Cuántos alumnos hay en tu clase?

—Cuarenta. Es lo normal en España. Curso el tercero de BUP. El año que viene, si apruebo, hago el COU antes de ir a la universidad.
—¿A qué hora empiezan las clases?
—A las ocho y media, y cada clase dura una hora. Pero hoy no tengo nada hasta las nueve y media.
—¿No debes asistir al Instituto cuando no tienes clase?
—No. Y como soy externa, vuelvo a casa para comer. Comemos a las tres.
—¿No hay clases por la tarde?
—Sí, hombre. Desde las cuatro y media hasta las siete, con media hora de recreo, cuando podemos ir a tomar un bocadillo o un café en el bar.
—¿Me has dicho en el bar? ¿El Instituto tiene un bar?
—Claro.
—Qué bien. Qué suerte tenéis.
—Suerte, no. Esta semana tengo evaluaciones. Si no saco buenas notas, si me suspenden, tendré que repetir el año que viene. Tengo que estudiar esta tarde, pero tú me ayudarás con el inglés.
—¿Cómo son tus profesores?
—El tutor es el profesor de inglés. Es estricto, pero sus clases son muy divertidas. Es muy simpático; le respetamos todos. En cambio, la profesora de informática es muy severa y exigente, nos castiga sin motivo y la odiamos todos.

Vocabulary

¡qué va! nothing of the kind, nonsense
el curso school year
a fines de at the end of
las Navidades Christmas period
la Semana Santa week before Easter Sunday
es lo normal it's the normal thing
el tercero de BUP final year of bachillerato (school-leaving qualification)
si apruebo if I pass
el COU pre-university year
asistir a to attend, be present at
externo, -na day pupil, (goes home for lunch)
qué suerte tenéis how lucky you are

las evaluaciones assessment (instead of public examinations, Spain has annual school assessments)
si no saco buenas notas if I don't get good marks
si me suspenden if I fail
repetir to repeat the year
el tutor, la tutora form teacher
le respetamos todos we all respect him
la informática computer studies
es muy severa y exigente she is very strict and demanding
nos castiga sin motivo she punishes us for no reason

Other Useful Vocabulary

mi profesor ...	my teacher ...
... explica bien/mal	... explains things well/badly
... tiene genio	... is bad tempered
... es aburrido	... is boring
... hace la vista gorda	... turns a blind eye

Mi profesor hace la vista gorda.

la economía me cuesta mucho trabajo	I find economics very hard
lo encuentro muy fácil/difícil	I find it very easy/difficult
saber de memoria	to learn by heart
repasar los apuntes	to revise notes
merezco salir bien/mal en	I deserve to do well/badly in
estoy flojo, -ja en	I'm weak in
estoy fuerte en	I'm good at
estudiar ...	to study ...
... el comercio	... business studies
... el hogar	... domestic science/home economics
... los trabajos manuales	... CDT
la asignatura obligatoria/optativa	compulsory/optional subject
sobresaliente	grade A
pasar lista	to take the register
faltar (a una clase)	to be absent (from a lesson)
la justificación	absence note
hacer novillos	to play truant
portarse bien/mal	to behave well/badly
regañar } reñir }	to tell off
la formación profesional	vocational training
el interno, la interna	boarder
el/la mediopensionista	pupil staying for lunch

Likes and Dislikes
Gustar
What you like becomes the subject (though it often follows the verb) and the person doing the liking becomes the indirect object. English says 'he likes skiing'; Spanish says 'to him is pleasing skiing'. *Gustar* can only be used in the third person singular or plural, depending on whether what you like is singular or plural.

e.g. *Me gusta la historia.*
(to me is pleasing history)
I like history.

But: *Me gustan las matemáticas.* (plural)
(to me are pleasing mathematics)
I like mathematics.

Les gusta bordar.
(to them is pleasing to embroider)
They like to embroider.

But: *Les gustan los bombones.* (plural)
(to them are pleasing chocolates)
They like chocolates.

When the Object Is a Noun
Personal *a* is needed, and the indirect object pronoun is used AS WELL.

e.g. *A mi tía le gustan los gatos.*   My aunt likes cats.
A los franceses les gusta el vino.   Frenchmen like wine.

To Emphasise the Pronoun
When you want to stress the subject and it is a pronoun (I like beef, but they like chicken), use *a* before the strong form of the pronoun, followed by the indirect object pronoun.

e.g. *A mí me gustan los idiomas, pero a ella le gusta más la química.*   I like languages, but she likes chemistry better.

Vocabulary: Approval

me gusta(n) más ... I like ... better	**me divierto dibujando** I amuse myself by drawing
me divierte(n) (Like **gustar**) ... ... amuse(s) me	**me relajo tocando la guitarra** I relax playing the guitar
me hace(n) reír/llorar (Like **gustar**) ... ... make(s) me laugh/cry	**pasamos un buen rato** we had a good time
me apasiona(n) (Like **gustar**) ... I'm mad about ...	**¡qué bien!** how nice!

Likes and Dislikes

es/me parece ...	it's/I think it's ...
... apasionante	... thrilling
... estupendo, -da	... marvellous
... extraordinario, -ria	... extraordinary
... fenomenal	... fantastic
... genial	... brilliant
... sensacional	... sensational
... tremendo, -da	... terrific

Vocabulary: Disapproval

no me gusta(n) nada I don't like it (them) at all
me da(n) asco (Like **gustar**) it (they) disgust(s) me
detesto I detest
odio I hate
estoy harto, -ta de I'm fed up with
no aguanto I can't stand
no puedo con I can't cope with
no puedo más I can't stand any more
lo pasé mal I had a rotten time
pasé un mal rato I had a bad time
¡tonterías! rubbish!
¡qué horror! how awful!
qué feo, fea how ugly
en absoluto not one bit

Pasé un mal rato.

es/me parece ...	it's/I think it's ...
... malo, -la	... bad
... asqueroso, -sa	... disgusting
... atroz	... awful
... aburrido, -da	... boring
... espantoso, -sa	... appalling
... fatal	... rotten, awful
... ridículo, -la	... ridiculous

- 'How ...!' is ¡*Qué* ...!
   e.g. ¡*Qué asco!* How revolting!
   ¡*Qué interesante!* How interesting!

Vocabulary: Surprise

¡qué cosa más rara! how extraordinary!
¡qué raro! how odd!
¡qué cosas dices! the things you say!
¡lo que son las cosas! imagine that!
es increíble it's incredible
parece mentira well I never!
¡qué sorpresa! what a surprise!
¡Dios mío! good gracious!
¡por Dios! for heaven's sake!
¡no me digas! you don't say!
¡qué barbaridad! how awful!
¡caray! wow, gosh!
¡caramba! dear me!
¡hombre! good heavens! (can express many emotions)
eso me extraña I'm surprised at that
no me extraña verla aquí I'm not surprised to see her here

Writing Formal Letters

1. The town you are writing from and the date go on the same line in the top right-hand corner — *Swansea, 9 de diciembre de 1990*.
2. Begin: *Muy señor mío:* (to a man)   *Muy señora mía:* (to a woman)
3. End: *Le saluda atentamente* or *Atentamente*, and sign your full name below.

Javier's Job Application

Sevilla, 31 de marzo de 1991

Muy señor mío:

Tengo dieciocho años y nací en Sevilla el 26 de febrero de 1973. Actualmente curso el COU en el Instituto Miguel de Cervantes, pero he decidido no presentarme a la selectividad, sino de buscar empleo.

Deseo solicitar la plaza de agente de ventas. Hablo y escribo bien el inglés, y me gustaría trabajar en contacto con el público. Les adjunto referencias escritas por el director del Instituto y del cura, que me conoce desde hace diez años.

Si quiere entrevistarme o necesita más información, estoy a su disposición. En espera de sus noticias le saluda atentamente

Javier Martínez

Javier Martínez García

'And' and 'Or' · Avoiding the Subjunctive

Vocabulary

actualmente now	**adjunto referencias** I enclose
cursar to study	references
presentarse a un examen to sit an	**el director** headmaster
examination	**el cura** parish priest
la selectividad university	**estoy a su disposición** I am at
entrance test	your service
deseo solicitar la plaza de I want	**en espera de sus noticias**
to apply for the post of	awaiting your reply
el agente de ventas salesman	
trabajar en contacto con el	
público to work with people	

Useful Phrases

en relación con el anuncio en	with reference to the advertisement
La Vanguardia de hoy...	in today's La Vanguardia...
estoy disponible desde principios	I am available from the beginning
de julio	of July

'And' and 'Or'

Whenever the following word begins with *i-* or *hi-* (but not *hie-*), 'and' is not *y* but *e*.

e.g. *Van a visitar Francia e Inglaterra.* They're going to visit France and England.

Padre e hijo. Father and son.

But: *Lo prefiero con limón y hielo.* I prefer it with lemon and ice.

Similarly, when the next word begins with *o-* or *ho-*, 'or' becomes *u*.

e.g. *Voy a apuntarlo en seguida u olvidaré hacerlo.* I'll note it down at once or I'll forget to do it.

Avoiding the Subjunctive

After verbs expressing emotion, wanting somebody to do something, and *cuando* referring to the future, the subjunctive is required. It is easier to avoid it.

a) Use *después de* + infinitive, instead of *cuando*:

Después de llegar a casa, tomaré un té. When I get home, I'll have a cup of tea.

b) Use *al* + infinitive, 'on doing something':

Al volver a España me escribirá. When he gets back to Spain he'll write to me.

c) Use two short sentences instead of one:
Tengo que hacerlo. Mi padre lo quiere. I have to do it. My father wants me to.
No puedes venir. ¡Qué lástima! You can't come. What a pity.
Me dices que tu madre está enferma. Lo siento mucho. You say your mother's ill. I'm so sorry.
d) When the subject is the same, *sentir* + infinitive can be used (but if you are sorry that he can't come, the subjunctive is needed):
Siente mucho no haberte visto ayer. She's very sorry she didn't see you yesterday.

The Listening Test

Practise by listening to Spanish on the radio, TV, cassettes or by listening to Spaniards themselves. Get pen-friends to record cassettes about themselves, their family, school, holiday, etc.

Don't try to understand every word. Train yourself to catch times, dates, or words relating to the question, and let the rest flow past you.

Hints

1. Check whether the item will be read twice.
2. Read the question before the recording starts. Time is allowed for this.
3. You should have plenty of time to write your answer. For short items, listen to both recordings before answering. Note down key facts, then write your answer in full.
4. Give necessary facts only — e.g. answer 'Where will you meet?' by 'Outside the cinema at 7 p.m.', not 'He asked me to meet him outside the cinema at seven o'clock'.
5. Write numbers as figures: 10 January 1985. Practise writing numbers — ask a friend to read them out to you.
6. Include all relevant details. If the weather forecast is *un día soleado con temperaturas muy altas*, it is NOT enough to answer 'What will the weather be like?' by 'sunny', 'hot' or 'good'. You must say both 'hot' and 'sunny'.
7. Guess intelligently. 'A wall two miles high' is NOT likely, 'a wall two metres high' is.
8. Always write something as an answer. You may get some marks, whereas you will certainly get none if you leave a blank.

Listening Practice

1. While you are alone in the house, you have to take a telephone message for your Spanish friend's mother. Write down, in English, the main points you must remember to tell her when she gets back (there are three).
2. (Higher level) You hear a programme on Spanish radio in which a bullfighter talks about his job. Draw up a list, in English, of what seem to you the main advantages and disadvantages about his job.

Answers:
1. (a) Her glasses are ready/at the shop (b) She can collect them tomorrow (c) Take the receipt.
2. For: He gets applause, worship, girls throw flowers to him, shouts of admiration, can earn a lot of money.

Against: Public forgets you if not successful, lonely in bullring, short life, retire young, dangerous, hard work, rushes from fair to fair, sometimes sleeps in train, not home at night, doesn't see much of children, if injured can spend months in hospital.

Speaking Practice

1. You are talking to your Spanish friend about your plans for the future. You begin:
   a) Ask what she intends to do next year.
   I'm going to study computer science. What about you?
   b) Tell her you want to work in a bank.
   Don't you want to go to university?
   c) Say you're not sure — it depends if you pass your exams.
   What are your favourite subjects?
   d) Say you like maths and physics best.
2. (Higher level) You've applied for a summer job on a camp site in Spain, and the owner is interviewing you:
   Do you speak Spanish well?
   a) Say you've been learning it for five years.
   Have you had a job before?
   b) Say you used to work in a shoe-shop on Saturdays.
   What are your plans for next year?
   c) Tell him you want to go back to school to study languages.
   When can you start?
   d) After term ends, on 20 July.

An Eventful Outing

5 A Day Out

This chapter deals with filling-stations and breakdowns, with different ways of travelling and with buying a train ticket. It revises names of countries, how to say you have just done something, the preterite tense and using 'must', 'ought' and 'need'. There is a check-list of past tenses to help you decide which to use, and there is a Higher level speaking practice with hints on how to tackle it.

An Eventful Outing

El sábado, los Martínez decidieron llevar a Sarah a Córdoba. Primero el señor Martínez fue a una gasolinera para llenar el depósito.

—Buenos días, señor. ¿Qué desea, súper o normal?

—Póngame veinte litros de súper. Y luego hágame el favor de limpiar el parabrisas y comprobar la presión de los neúmaticos; hoy vamos a Córdoba.

—¿Le compruebo el aceite también?

—Sí.

• • • • •

Media hora más tarde, el señor Martínez paró el coche.

—¿Qué te pasa?

—Tenemos un pinchazo.

Tenemos un pinchazo.

—Dios mío, ¿qué vamos a hacer?

—Pues, nada, mujer. Voy a poner la rueda de repuesto.

Pero después de cambiar la rueda, el coche no arrancó. El señor Martínez se enfadó.

—Llevé el coche al taller la semana pasada; les dije que no iba bien.

—¿Por qué no volvemos a la estación de servicio?

—Porque allí no hay taller. Menos mal que acabamos de pasar un teléfono.

• • • • •

—Talleres San Mauricio. Dígame.

—Buenos días. Mi coche está averiado. No arranca. ¿Puede enviarme

un mecánico? Estoy en la carretera nacional a media hora de Sevilla, dirección de Córdoba.
—¿No se ha quedado Vd. sin gasolina?
—Claro que no, acabo de llenar el depósito.
—Le puedo enviar una grúa para remolcarle al taller. ¿Qué marca tiene el coche?
—No, no necesitamos grúa. Un mecánico lo arreglará en seguida. Es un Seat.
—Muy bien, no se preocupe. Llegará un mecánico dentro de una hora.

Vocabulary

la gasolinera petrol station	**el motor** engine
la estación de servicio service station	**¿no se ha quedado sin gasolina?** you haven't run out of petrol?
el taller garage with repair workshop	**la grúa** breakdown lorry
llenar el depósito fill the tank	**remolcar** to tow
limpiar el parabrisas clean the windscreen	**la marca** make, brand
comprobar... to check...	**no se preocupe** don't worry
...**los neumáticos** ...the tyres	**lo arreglará en seguida** he'll mend it at once
...**el aceite** ...the oil	**sin plomo** unleaded
¿qué te pasa? what's wrong?	**la matrícula** car registration number
tener un pinchazo to have a puncture	**las horas punta** rush hour
la rueda de repuesto spare wheel	**el atasco** } traffic jam
no arrancó it didn't start	**el embotellamiento**
no iba bien it wasn't going well	**poner una multa** to fine
menos mal (que) luckily	**un coche de ocasión** second-hand car
está averiado,-da it's broken down	**el permiso de conducir** driving-licence
la avería breakdown	

Buying a Rail Ticket

Al día siguiente, Elena llevó a Sarah a la oficina de la RENFE en Sevilla para sacar billetes. Buscaron el letrero que decía 'Largo recorrido. Venta anticipada.'
—Buenos días. Quisiera dos billetes para Málaga para pasado mañana. ¿Hay un tren a eso de las ocho?
—A ver. Sí, hay un TER a las ocho diez. O un rápido a las nueve

57

menos cinco. Quedan billetes para los dos. ¿Los quiere de ida y vuelta o sólo de ida?

—Nos da dos billetes de ida y vuelta para el TER. De segunda clase, y si es posible en un departamento de no fumadores, al lado de la ventanilla. ¿Es directo?

—No, hay que hacer transbordo en Bobadilla.

—¿Tenemos que reservar un asiento?

—No, la reserva de asiento va incluida.

—¿Cuánto le debo?

—Un momento. Como no es día azul, les va a costar más. Y hay un suplemento para el TER.

Vocabulary

sacar billetes	to buy tickets	**¿es directo?**	is it a through train?
el letrero	notice, sign	**hay que hacer transbordo**	you have to change
largo recorrido	long distance		
venta anticipada	advance sales	**la reserva de asiento va incluida**	the seat reservation is included
un billete de ida y vuelta	return		
la RENFE	Spanish railways	**el día azul**	cheap travel day
el rápido	train stopping at big towns only	**el jefe de tren**	guard
		el revisor	ticket collector
el TER	air-conditioned express	**la litera**	couchette, berth
el TALGO	luxury inter-city train	**¿está ocupado?**	is it taken?
a ver	let's see	**... libre?**	... free?
un departamento de no fumadores	non-smoking compartment	**con destino a**	going to
		procedente de	coming from
al lado de la ventanilla	next to the window	**viene con retraso**	is late
¿de qué andén sale el próximo tren para Santander?		what platform does the next train for Santander leave from?	
con motivo de la huelga convocada por el personal ...		because of the strike by employees ...	

Transport Vocabulary
Land

el cobrador	bus conductor	**¿quiere Vd. avisarme cuando lleguemos a ...?**	will you tell me when we get to ...?
el conductor	driver		
el bono-bus	cheap ticket		
la boca del metro	entrance to Metro	**tengo que bajar en la parada siguiente**	I have to get off at the next stop

Sea

el hidroala	hovercraft	**el camarote**	cabin
la travesía	crossing	**el crucero**	cruise
el Canal de la Mancha	English Channel	**marearse**	to be seasick

Air

facturar	to check in	**aterrizar** ⎫	to land
embarcar	to board	**tomar tierra** ⎭	
la tarjeta de embarque	boarding card	**abrocharse el cinturón de seguridad**	to fasten one's seat-belt
la lista de espera	waiting-list		
el comandante	captain (of plane)	**libre de impuestos**	duty-free
la tripulación	crew	**pasar por la aduana**	to go through customs
despegar	to take off		

Geography

1. Most countries do <u>not</u> need the definite article.
   Inglaterra limita con Gales y Escocia.   England has borders with Wales and Scotland.
2. These countries need the article:
el Canadá	Canada
los Estados Unidos (EE.UU.)	United States (USA)
la Argentina	Argentina
el Brasil	Brazil
el Perú	Peru
las Antillas	West Indies
la India	India
el Japón	Japan

   <u>El</u> Brasil es célebre por su Carnaval.   Brazil is famous for its Carnival.
   Vamos <u>al</u> Japón en enero.   We're going to Japan in January.
   Es de <u>las</u> Antillas.   S/he's from the West Indies.
3. <u>All</u> countries used with an adjective or adjectival phrase need the article.
la <u>Gran</u> Bretaña	Great Britain
la América <u>del Norte</u>	North America
la España <u>de Franco</u>	Franco's Spain
4. The same word is normally the adjective, the inhabitant and the language: a <u>French</u> book, a <u>Frenchman</u> and the <u>French language</u> are all *francés*.

5. *El* is used before a language except after the verb *hablar* or its subject.
Thus: *Hablan griego.* They speak Greek.
¿Habla Vd. ruso? Do you speak Russian?
But: *Guillermo habla muy bien el italiano.* Guillermo speaks Italian very well.
¿Crees que es más difícil el turco que el polaco? Do you think Turkish is more difficult than Polish?

To Have Just Done Something

Only two tenses are possible with *acabar de* + infinitive.

a)

English 'have just'	Spanish present tense
We have just seen him	*Acabamos de verle*

b)

English 'had just'	Spanish imperfect tense
We had just seen him	*Acabábamos de verle*

Necessity (Must, Ought, Need)

1. 'Tener que' + Infinitive

'To have to':
Tiene que coger el avión en Londres. He has to catch the plane in London.

2. 'Deber' + Infinitive

'Must':
No debes dejar Nerja sin visitar a tus tíos. You mustn't leave Nerja without visiting your aunt and uncle.

3. 'Deber de' + Infinitive

'Must' meaning 'suppose':
Debe de ser su nieto. It must be (I suppose it is) his grandson.
Deben de haber perdido el tren. They must have (I expect they've) missed the train.

4. 'Haber de' + Infinitive

Weaker than (1) and (2), 'to be supposed to':
He de empezar mañana. I'm to start tomorrow.

Necessity (Must, Ought, Need)

5. **'Hay que' + Infinitive**

   Used only in third person singular, 'one has to':
   Hay que entrenarse para ser buen futbolista. You have to train if you want to be a good footballer.

6. **'Es preciso' + Infinitive**

   Used only in third person singular, 'it is necessary':
   Fue preciso alquilar un coche. It was necessary (I/we/he/they had) to hire a car.

7. **'Necesitar'**

   'To need':
   Necesitaban gasolina. They needed petrol.
   Vd. no necesitará un diccionario. You won't need a dictionary.

8. **'Hacer falta'**

   'To need'; like *gustar* (Chapter 4) what you need becomes the subject of *hacer* and the person who needs it becomes the indirect object:
   Nos hace falta una mochila. We need a rucksack. (*mochila* singular, so *hace*)

   Nos hace falta una mochila.

   Me hacen falta seis pañuelos. I need six handkerchiefs. (*pañuelos* plural, so *hacen*)

9. **'Faltar'**

   'To be lacking', 'to be short of' (like *gustar*):
   Nos falta jabón. We need soap. (*jabón* singular, so *falta*)
   ¿Cuántas toallas te faltan? How many towels are you short of? (*toallas* plural, so *faltan*)

61

The Preterite

This tense is used for a single finished action in the past. English uses 'I talked', 'I did talk', 'did you talk?' and 'I did not talk'.
- Spanish uses only ONE word, and does not translate 'did'.

Formation for Regular Verbs

Remove *-ar*, *-er* or *-ir* from the infinitive and add endings.

<u>comp</u>*rar*			<u>beber</u> and *-ir* verbs like *vi<u>v</u>ir*		
compr	*é*	I bought	*beb*	*í*	I drank
compr	*aste*	you bought	*beb*	*iste*	you drank
compr	*ó*	s/he, you(*Vd.*)bought	*beb*	*ió*	s/he, you(*Vd.*)drank
compr	*amos*	we bought	*beb*	*imos*	we drank
compr	*asteis*	you bought	*beb*	*isteis*	you drank
compr	*aron*	they, you(*Vds.*)bought	*beb*	*ieron*	they, you(*Vds.*)drank

Formation for Radical Changing Verbs

The preterite of *-ar* and *-er* verbs has <u>no vowel change</u>. Radical changing verbs in *-ir* change *o* to *u*, and *e* to *i*, in the <u>third person singular and plural only</u>.

e.g.

dormir		*pedir*	
dormí	I slept	*pedí*	I asked for
dormiste	you slept	*pediste*	you asked for
d<u>u</u>rmió	s/he, you(*Vd.*)slept	*p<u>i</u>dió*	s/he, you(*Vd.*)asked for
dormimos	we slept	*pedimos*	we asked for
dormisteis	you slept	*pedisteis*	you asked for
d<u>u</u>rmieron	they, you(*Vds.*) slept	*p<u>i</u>dieron*	they, you(*Vds.*)asked for

Spelling Changes: First Person Singular

a) Infinitive ends in *-car*, *c* becomes *qu*.
   e.g. *buscar   bus<u>qu</u>é, buscaste,* etc.
b) Infinitive ends in *-gar*, *g* becomes *gu*.
   e.g. *llegar   lle<u>gu</u>é, llegaste,* etc.
c) Infinitive ends in *-zar*, *z* becomes *c*.
   e.g. *empezar   empe<u>c</u>é, empezaste,* etc.

Spelling Changes: Third Person Singular and Plural

Infinitive ends in *-aer*, *-eer*, *-oír*, *-uir*, *-oer*; *i* becomes *y*.
   e.g. *leer*
      leí   I read
      leiste   you read

The Preterite

leyó	s/he, you(*Vd.*)read
leímos	we read
leísteis	you read
leyeron	they, you(*Vds.*)read

Irregular Verbs

The following verbs have no accent on the first person singular ending and the third person singular is -*o* not -*ió*.

a) *Ir* and *ser* have the same preterite. There is no confusion as *el restaurante donde fuimos ayer* must mean 'the restaurant where we went yesterday'. 'The restaurant where we were yesterday' would be *donde estuvimos* (*estar* for position).

fui	I was or I went
fuiste	etc.
fue	
fuimos	
fuisteis	
fueron	

b) Endings in -*u*- are as follows:

tener

tuve	I had
tuviste	etc.
tuvo	
tuvimos	
tuvisteis	
tuvieron	

Like *tener* are:

estar	*estuve*	I was
andar	*anduve*	I walked
conducir	*conduje*	I drove
poder	*pude*	I could
poner	*puse*	I put
saber	*supe*	I knew

c) Endings in -*i*- are as follows:

dar

di	I gave
diste	etc.
dio	
dimos	
disteis	
dieron	

decir

dije	I said
dijiste	etc.
dijo	
dijimos	
dijisteis	
dijeron	

Also ending in -*i*- are:

hacer	*hice*	I did, made
querer	*quise*	I wanted
venir	*vine*	I came
ver	*vi*	I saw

hizo s/he, you did, made

- Compound verbs ending in any of the above verbs will have the same preterite ending.

  e.g. *contener* (to contain), *contuve*
  suponer (to suppose), *supuse*

The Preterite in Conversation

It is vital to stress the right vowel when speaking. If you don't, a Spaniard will understand something completely different.

e.g. *Tomo el recado.* (first *o* stressed) I'm taking or I'll take the message. (first person singular, present tense)
Tomó el recado. (second *o* stressed) S/he took the message. (third person singular, preterite)
Pase tres días en Mallorca. (*a* stressed) Go and spend three days in Mallorca. (imperative, an order)
Pasé tres días en Mallorca. (stressing *é*) I spent three days in Mallorca. (first person singular, preterite)

Which Past Tense?

1. Uses of the Preterite

a) For a series of events in the past, each taking the story one stage further:
Llegué al Instituto, me quité el abrigo, entré en la clase y me senté al lado de mi mejor amigo.
I arrived at school, took off my coat, went into the class-room and sat down next to my best friend.

b) For events seen as completed and now belonging to the past:
La Guerra Civil empezó en 1936 y duró tres años.
The Civil War began in 1936 and lasted for three years.

2. Uses of the Perfect (Chapter 7)

For recently completed actions in the past:
He cambiado de idea. I've changed my mind.

3. Uses of the Imperfect (Chapter 6)

(English 'they wore', 'they were wearing', 'they used to wear')

a) For a habit in the past:
Cada día cogíamos el tren a las siete. Every day we caught the train at seven/we used to catch the train at seven.

b) For repeated action in the past:
Hablábamos alemán a los austriacos cuando venían a casa.

We spoke German to the Austrians when they came to the house. (i.e. the Austrians came <u>more than once</u>)

c) For an action going on in the background when another event occurred:
<u>Leía</u> el periódico cuando el cartero llegó. I was reading the paper when the postman arrived.

d) For descriptions in the past:
<u>Llevabas</u> un vestido blanco cuando te conocí, ¿te acuerdas?
You were wearing a white dress when I first met you, do you remember?

4. Uses of the Pluperfect (Chapter 8)

For an event <u>further back in the past</u> than the action of the main verb:
Porque <u>había terminado</u> mis deberes, mi padre me dejó salir.
Because I had finished my homework, my father let me go out.

Listening Practice

1. Waiting for a plane at the airport, you hear your flight announced.
   a) What does the announcement tell you?
   b) What must you do if you have a brown card?
   c) Your card is green. What are you told?

2. (Higher level) While staying in Alicante, you hear this report on the radio about road conditions. You know your Spanish friend's father is going to Valencia today, so you note down in English where he may have problems.

Answers:
1. (a) Flight now boarding through Gate no. 7   (b) Go at once to Gate no. 7   (c) Stay in waiting-room until next announcement.
2. (a) North of Alicante, 3 kilometres of roadworks   (b) Near Benidorm, rush-hour queues of stationary cars   (c) Entering Valencia, bottle-neck, and can take 1½ hours to get into city.

Speaking Practice

1. You are on holiday in Jávea, and on Saturday you decide to hire a car for the day. You go to the hotel receptionist to ask about car hire.
You begin:
   a) Ask if there's a car hire company in Jávea.
   There is, but it's closed on Saturday.

Speaking Practice

   b) Ask if there's anywhere near Jávea where you could hire a car.
   Well, there's an ATESA office in Benidorm.
   c) Ask how far Benidorm is.
   About fifty kilometres, but there's a good bus service.
   d) Ask her to give you the address and telephone number of the Benidorm company.

2. (Higher level) This is a more difficult open-ended exercise. It is not set out as a dialogue and you may have to deal with the unexpected.
   a) You saw this card advertising a taxi firm in the hotel Miramar where you are staying. You ring them up, and a man answers.
   b) Book a taxi for 8 a.m. tomorrow to take you to the airport.
   c) Ask how much it will cost, and answer any questions you are asked.

Read on <u>before</u> attempting the role-play.

> **TELETAXI**
> *Servicio por teléfono*
> *24 horas al día*
> 71 33 24 19
> Coches para bodas y excursiones turísticas. Reservas anticipadas.
> Se admiten tarjetas de crédito.

Imagine the real-life situation. What must you tell the taxi firm?
   —the name of your hotel
   —the time you want the taxi
   —where you want to go to

There will be questions, so plan ahead. Obviously they'll ask your name, and possibly how to spell it. They may want the number of passengers, whether it's an international flight, the time the plane leaves. Prepare your answers. Now do the role-play <u>before</u> reading the next paragraph.

• • • • •

The last question is unexpected – where did you get our firm's name? In this case you have the answer: *en el hotel*, or *su tarjeta está en el hotel*. If you were not told the answer, name any obvious place such as *en la guía de teléfonos*, *en la oficina de turismo*, *en la recepción del hotel*, *en el periódico*, etc.

6 Booking a Camp Site or Hotel

This chapter revises booking at a camp site, writing to book rooms in a hotel, going skiing and holidays in general. There is a weather forecast with sample answers. Different ways of saying 'to stay', and 'hot' and 'cold' are explained, and the grammar section revises phrases using 'tener', adverbs, and the imperfect and continuous imperfect tenses.

Sarah Books a Camp Site

Unos amigos ingleses de Sarah, Terry y David, acaban de llegar a Sevilla y han telefoneado a Sarah para pedir su ayuda. Quieren pasar quince días en un camping, y no hablan español. Sarah monta detrás de David en su moto y los tres van al camping 'Las Arenas Doradas'.

—Buenos días, señor. Mis amigos no hablan español, y les he acompañado para hacer de intérprete. ¿Quedan plazas en el camping?
—Sí, señorita. ¿Para cuántos días?
—Quieren quedarse quince días.
—¿Y cuántas personas son?
—Dos.
—¿Con una coche y tienda, o con una caravana?
—No, con una moto y una tienda cada uno.
—¿Tienen algún documento de identidad?
—Llevan el carné de camping, o tienen pasaportes, si Vd. prefiere.
—No, con el carné está bien. Aquí tienen una lista de servicios a su disposición.

Las Arenas Doradas

SERVICIOS QUE PONE A SU DISPOSICIÓN	FACILITIES AVAILABLE
a) Sanitarios amplios	a) Spacious sanitary installations
b) Duchas de agua caliente gratuita	b) Free hot-water showers
c) Correo	c) Post
d) Snack-bar	d) Snack bar
e) Restaurante (menú del día)	e) Restaurant (set meals)
f) Platos para llevar a su tienda	f) Take-away meals
g) Supermercado (pan fresco cada día a las 8 h., venta de carne y comestibles)	g) Supermarket (fresh bread daily at 8 a.m., meat and groceries)
h) Venta de hielo	h) Ice-cubes sold

Sarah Books a Camp Site

i) Zona de juegos infantiles
j) Piscinas, ping-pong, petanca
k) Información turística (excursiones) en recepción
l) Posibilidad de pesca a 20 m del camping
m) Barbacoas a disposición de los clientes del camping en una zona ajardinada con mesa
n) Guardia de noche.

i) Children's playground
j) Swimming-pools, ping-pong, French bowls
k) Tourist information (excursions) at reception
l) Fishing available 20 m from campsite
m) Barbecues for campers, tables set in gardens
n) Night-watchman.

La barrera se cierra a los once, y todos los campistas tienen que respetar las reglas: no encender fuego, no tirar basura, no jugar al fútbol delante de la tienda, además de esta lista que tiene una traducción inglesa abajo.

NORMAS GENERALES DEL CAMPING
1. Prohibida la circulación en el interior del camping de las 12 horas de la noche a las 8 de la mañana.
2. Por favor, tengan cuidado con los árboles y plantas.
3. El lugar de acampada ha de quedar libre y limpio a las 12 horas del mediodía.
4. Se admiten perros, atados.
5. Si precisan de los servicios de guardia de noche por alguna urgencia, llamen al timbre situado en la puerta del bar.
6. Bajen el volumen de su receptor de radio o TV a las 11 horas de la noche.
7. Por favor, empleen adecuadamente los fregaderos para la vajilla y los lavaderos para la ropa.
8. Empleen los cubos para los desechos.
9. Por favor pasen por la ducha antes de entrar en la piscina.
   Gracias de antemano por su colaboración.

GENERAL RULES OF THE CAMP SITE
1. No traffic inside the site from midnight to 8 a.m.
2. Please be careful with trees and plants.
3. The camping place must be left clean and vacated by midday.
4. Dogs are allowed provided they are tied up.
5. If you need the night-watchman in an emergency, ring the bell beside the door of the Bar.

6. Turn down your radio or TV after 11 p.m.
7. Please use the proper sinks for washing up and for washing clothes.
8. Use the buckets provided for your garbage.
9. Please shower before entering the swimming pool.
   Thank you in advance for your co-operation.

Vocabulary

hacer de intérprete to act as interpreter
¿quedan plazas en el camping? are there places left in the camp site?
respetar las normas/reglas to obey the rules
no tirar basura don't throw rubbish around
montar la tienda to put up the tent
el saco de dormir sleeping bag
la linterna torch
el agua potable (f) drinking-water
el remolque caravan, trailer
el albergue juvenil youth hostel

Booking a Hotel

Sr. Director,
Hotel el Faro,
Matalascañas,
Sevilla.

            Sevilla, 15 de marzo de 1990.

Muy señor mío:

 Quisiera reservar tres habitaciones con baño y con pensión completa para una semana del 7 al 13 de abril. Necesitamos una habitación individual y dos dobles, una con cama de matrimonio y otra con dos camas, de preferencia con balcón y vista al mar.

 Viajamos en coche y pensamos llegar por la tarde, a eso de las seis, el día 7. Le agradecería recibir su confirmación lo antes posible.

 En espera de su respuesta, le saluda atentamente

       Rafael Martínez Morales

       Rafael Martínez Morales

Vocabulary

media pensión half board	**la cama de matrimonio** double bed
pensión completa full board	
una habitación individual single room	**de preferencia** preferably
	con vista al mar with sea view
una habitación doble double room	
le agradecería recibir su confirmación lo antes posible	I should be grateful if you would confirm (the booking) as soon as possible
en espera de su repuesta	looking forward to your reply

Holiday Vocabulary

tomar el sol to sunbathe	**el toldo** awning, sunshade
broncearse to tan	**la cuenta** bill
la arena sand	**la factura** account
la ola wave	**¿aceptan tarjetas de crédito?** do you take credit cards?
el faro lighthouse	
el acantilado cliff	**¿se admiten perros?** do you take dogs?
la gaviota seagull	
el quitasol beach umbrella	
no se admiten cheques personales, sólo eurocheques	personal cheques not accepted, only eurocheques.

To Stay

1. 'Quedarse' – To Remain

Maite se queda en casa.　Maite is staying at home.

Other Meanings:

Se quedó con mi bolígrafo.　He went off with my pen.

Sólo quedan cinco días para la fiesta.　There are only five days left to the party.

Quédese con el cambio.　Keep the change.

Me la/lo quedo.　I'll take it, buy it.

Nos hemos quedado sin dinero.　We've run out of money.

¿En qué quedamos?　What have we decided?

Hemos quedado con Pablo a las ocho.　We're meeting Pablo at eight.

2. 'Alojarse' – To Stay (hotel etc.)

Also *hospedarse.*

¿Dónde se aloja Vd.?　Where are you staying?

3. 'Visitar' – To Visit

¿Te gustaría visitarnos en Birmingham el verano que viene?
Would you like to come and stay with us in Birmingham next summer?

4. 'Pasar' + Length of Time – To Spend

Van a pasar la noche en casa de Alejandro. They're going to stay the night at Alejandro's.

The Weather

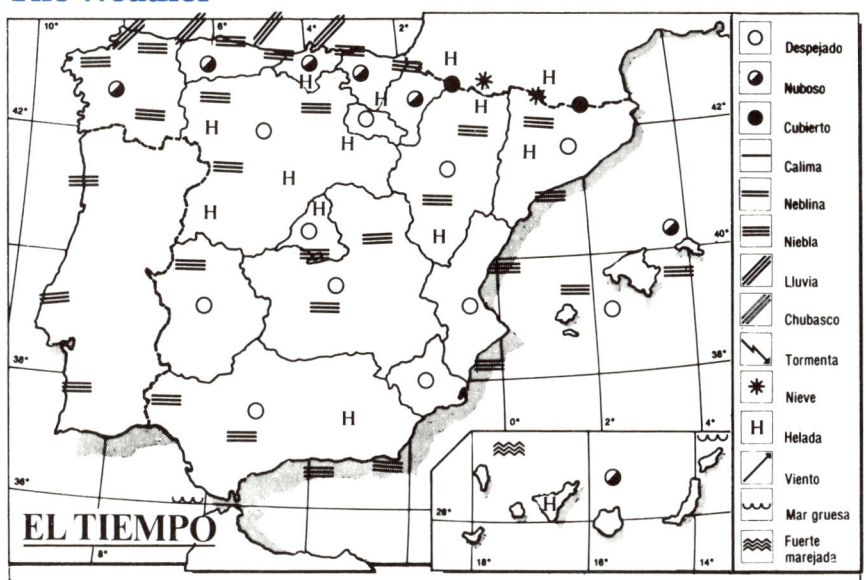

EL TIEMPO

O	Despejado
◐	Nuboso
●	Cubierto
═	Calima
≡	Neblina
≣	Niebla
╱╱	Lluvia
╱╱╱	Chubasco
⟍	Tormenta
✱	Nieve
H	Helada
╱	Viento
∿∿	Mar gruesa
≋	Fuerte marejada

Primaveral, excepto en el norte

ANDALUCIA. Continuará el cielo despejado en toda la comunidad. Nieblas por la mañana en el oeste y más persistentes en la costa mediterránea, incluido el Estrecho, Ceuta y Melilla. Vientos flojos del Este en Estrecho y muy flojos en el resto. Hielo en Sierra Nevada por encima de 1.900 metros. Suben las máximas en el oeste con 23° y mínimas de 0°.

CASTILLA – LA MANCHA Y EXTREMADURA. Continuará despejado. Bancos de niebla a primeras horas y calimas el resto del día. Calmas. Aumento de las máximas, con 21°, y mínimas de −2°.

CATALUÑA. Muy nuboso el Pirineo, con alguna nevada débil en la vertiente norte. Despejado en el resto, con nieblas, brisas costeras. Heladas débiles en el interior. Hielo en altitudes superiores a 1.800 metros. Máximas de 19° y mínimas de 0°.

The Weather

In both the reading test and the listening test you may be asked to show you understand a weather forecast (often called *la meteo*). A genuine forecast will give details of atmospheric pressure, cold fronts and anticyclones, depressions and so on. You will have to look for the sort of information you would need if planning a picnic, an outing or a day at the sea. Listen carefully for the <u>area</u> – several regions may be mentioned but you will only need to know about one.

Look for words that tell you it will <u>rain</u> (*precipitación, lluvia, llovizna, chubasco, tormenta*) or <u>snow</u> (*nieve, nevada, heladas*), or be <u>sunny</u> (*sol, despejado, grandes claros*).

See if the temperature is rising (*subida*) or falling (*bajada*). *Máximas* means the hottest, *mínimas* the coldest. The wind can be *fuerte* (strong) or *flojo* (light). *Débil* means 'light' or 'slight', e.g. *alguna nevada débil*, 'occasional light snowfalls'; or *heladas débiles en el interior*, 'slight frost inland'.

Sample Questions

1. *Would it be a good day to take a drive along the coast in Andalusia?*
Look for the key words. No rain, snow or frost, except above 1900 metres in the Sierra Nevada inland. The wind is *flojo* or *muy flojo*. There are *nieblas* in the morning in the West and on the Mediterranean coast, but otherwise *cielo despejado* and the temperatures rising to 23°.
<u>Answer</u> It would be a good day, with little wind, clear skies and pleasantly warm at 23°. The Atlantic coast might be better than the Mediterranean.

2. *Should you go climbing in the Pyrenees in Catalonia today?*
Little sun in the Pyrenees, plenty of cloud, and light snowfalls on the northern slopes. Freezing above 1800 metres (*hielo*). Inland and the coast are irrelevant, but *muy nuboso* sounds dangerous.
<u>Answer</u> With heavy cloud, the risk of light snowfalls and freezing temperatures, it is not a good day for mountain climbing.

Vocabulary

la llovizna drizzle	**la vertiente** slope
el claro clear period	**costero, -ra** coastal
el granizo hail	**soplar** to blow
la calima, calina haze	**la borrasca** squall
primaveral spring-like	**la nubosidad** cloud
el aumento increase	**la ola de frío/calor** cold spell/heatwave
hace 2 grados bajo cero it's 2 degrees below freezing	**el vendaval** gale

Talking About Weather

a) You can NEVER say *es/está mal tiempo* for 'the weather is bad'; ONLY *hace* mal tiempo.

b) Present tenses:
   llueve   it rains (in spring, often, in Blackpool)
   está lloviendo   it's raining (now, at this moment)

c) Three different verbs are needed to talk about weather: *hacer*, *estar*, and *hay* with nouns or adjectives; as well as verbs like *llover(ue)*, *tronar (ue)* (to thunder), *relampaguear* (to flash lightning), *granizar* (to hail), *nevar* (to snow).

Present (NOT Continuous)	Past	Future		
It is	It was	It will be		
hace	*hacía*	*hará*	*buen/mal tiempo* *calor/frío/fresco* *sol* *viento*	good/bad weather hot/cold/cool sunny windy
(For visible states of weather) *hay*	*había*	*habrá*	*neblina* *niebla* *chubascos* *tormenta*	misty foggy showery thundery
está	*estaba*	*estará*	*cubierto* *despejado* *nublado* *nuboso*	overcast cloudless cloudy cloudy

Hot and Cold

	verb	very	hot	cold	
1. People	*tengo* *tienes* etc. (agrees with subject)	*mucho*	*calor*	*frío*	I'm/you're etc. very hot/cold

	verb	very	hot	cold	
2. Weather	*hace* (never changes)	*mucho*	*calor*	*frío*	it's very hot/cold (weather)
3. Things (permanent state)	*es/son*	*muy*	*caliente(s)* (agrees)	*frío,-a(s)* (agrees)	it's/they're very hot/cold
4. Things (temporary state)	*está(n)*	*muy*	*caliente(s)* (agrees)	*frío,-a(s)* (agrees)	it's/they're very hot/cold

e.g. *Mi madre tiene mucho frío.* My mother's very cold.
Hace mucho calor en Ecija. It's very hot in Ecija.
El fuego es muy caliente. Fire is very hot. ⎫
La nieve es fría. Snow is cold. ⎬ (permanent state)
Estos cafés están fríos. These coffees are cold. ⎫ (tempor-
¡Ay! el agua está muy caliente. Ow! The water's very hot. ⎬ ary state)

Phrases with Tener

tengo dieciséis años I'm sixteen
tienes que afeitarte you must shave
tiene sueño s/he's sleepy
tenemos hambre we're hungry
tenéis sed you're thirsty
tienen frío they're cold
tengo calor I'm hot
tenemos ganas de salir we feel like going out

tienes prisa you're in a hurry
tiene razón s/he's right
Vd. tiene suerte you're lucky
tenemos éxito we're successful
tenéis cuidado you're careful
tienen vergüenza they're ashamed
Vds. tienen miedo you're afraid

- *Tener* is followed by a noun. To say someone is <u>very</u> hungry, use *mucho,-cha* not *muy*, and it will agree with the noun.

  e.g. *Tengo mucho sueño.* I'm very sleepy.
  Tienen mucha hambre. They're very hungry.
  Tiene muchas ganas de conocerte. S/he's very keen to meet you.

Javier's Ski Trip

Javier estaba muy alegre porque al día siguiente iba al Pirineo Aragonés a seguir un cursillo de esquí. Iba con el Instituto en viaje de fin de curso. Le mostró a Sarah el folleto que le habían dado en la Oficina de Turismo y el programa de 'Aprés Ski'. Sarah se rió mucho cuando leyó que había profesores en la estación de esquí, pero Javier no. Le dijo que no era broma, y que si tenía clases de matemáticas o de inglés, volvería a casa en seguida.

Javier's Leaflet

Après Ski

Domingo
- Bienvenida.
- Entrega dossier con detalle de actividades e información general.
- Entrega talonario de utilización de servicios.

Lunes
- Comienzo del cursillo.
- Proyección de películas de ski.
- Copa de recepción.

Martes
- Iniciación campeonatos (mus, parchís, dardos, etc.).
- Gran fiesta infantil.
- Concurso de muñecos de nieve.
- Cine comercial.
- Concurso de baile.

Miércoles
- Cine comercial.
- Descenso de antorchas (con participación de cursillistas).
- Queimada.
- Baile de disfraces.
- Proyección video de clases de ski.

Jueves
- Cine comercial.
- Recorrido mesones y valle.
- Elección de Miss y Míster cursillo.
- Bingo blanco.

Viernes
- Slalom cursillistas.
- Entrega de trofeos y diplomas. Resultados.
- Cocktail de despedida (sopas).

Servicios en la Estación

Todos los servicios que precise, están a su disposición:
Tenis ● Frontón ● Equitación ● Squash ● Guarderías infantiles ● Servicio canguro ● Discotecas ● Cine ● Restaurantes ● Tiendas de todo tipo ● Pubs ● Venta, reparación y alquiler de esquís.

Si sus hijos no pueden dejar de estudiar, disponemos de profesores para ayudarles y si usted no puede dejar totalmente el trabajo, ponemos a su disposición telex, secretarias, intérpretes, etc.

Autobús a la Telecabina

Tendrá a su disposición autobuses desde la urbanización al pie de la telecabina. El servicio se efectúa desde las 9 de la mañana hasta media hora después del cierre de pistas.

Servicios en Pistas

● Cafeterías y restaurante-autoservicio ● Alquiler y guardaesquís ● Venta de material complementario de ski ● Jardín de nieve ● Ski-helicóptero.

El mejor servicio de pistas es el equipo de profesionales que le preparan la mejor nieve.

Remontes

● 1 TELECABINA
● 4 TELESILLAS
● 12 TELESQUIS

Adverbs

Vocabulary

el cursillo (short) course	**el viaje de fin de curso** end-of-year school trip
la bienvenida welcome	**la estación de esquí** ski resort
el talonario book of vouchers	**no es broma** it's no joke
la copa de recepción welcoming drink	**el frontón** pelota court
la iniciación start	**la guardería infantil** day nursery
el campeonato championship	**servicio canguro** babysitting service
los dardos darts	**el alquiler de esquís** ski hire
el concurso de muñecos de nieve snowman contest	**el cierre** closing (down)
el/la cursillista student (on course)	**autoservicio** self-service
la antorcha flaming torch	**el/la debutante** beginner
el baile de disfraces fancy-dress ball	**el monitor, el instructor** ski instructor
la entrega de trofeos prize-giving	**la pista** ski-run
la despedida farewell	**el remonte** ski-lift
el puesto de socorro first-aid post	**la telecabina** cable-car
el esquí de fondo cross-country skiing	**el telesilla** chair-lift
	el telesquí ski tow
	el teleférico cable-car

Adverbs

Adverbs describe the action of a verb – they tell you <u>how</u> something was done.

1. Formation

Adverbs are formed from the feminine form of the adjective + *-mente*. If there is no feminine form, add *-mente* to the masculine.

Masculine		Feminine		Adverb	
inquieto	worried	*inquieta*	+ *-mente*	*inquietamente*	worriedly
fácil	easy	(same)	+ *-mente*	*fácilmente*	easily

2. Position

Normally the adverb comes <u>immediately after</u> the verb.

Habló <u>muy bien</u> de sus aventuras en Bolivia.
   verb   adverb

He spoke about his adventures in Bolivia <u>very well</u>.
  verb   adverb

Encontramos <u>fácilmente</u> la casa.   We found the house <u>easily</u>.
   verb   adverb   verb   adverb

3. Two or More Adverbs Used Together

Drop *-mente* from all but the last, but keep the feminine form of the adjectives.

Los dos hombres entraron rápida y silenciosamente. The two men entered quickly and silently.

4. Alternatives

a) *Con* + noun. This is used when adding *-mente* to a long adjective would make it clumsy.
Abrieron el paquete con cuidado. They opened the parcel carefully.

b) Use an adjective. It must agree with the subject of the verb.
Contestaron tímidos y respetuosos. They answered shyly and respectfully.

5. Other Forms

Some common adverbs do not end in *-mente*.

bien	well	*pronto*	soon	*temprano*	early
mal	badly	*despacio*	slowly	*tarde*	late

6. Very, Quite

Muy and *bastante* are used in front of an adverb.
Las mujeres salieron muy despacio. The women left very slowly.
Este autor escribe bastante bien. This author writes quite well.

The Imperfect Tense

Used for an action in the past when there is no precise moment at which it took place.

English equivalents:
 a) was/were . . . -ing
 b) used to . . .
 c) would . . .
 d) simple past tense – did, said, went, . . . -ed. This could be the preterite, but if you could use 'was . . . -ing' or 'used to . . . ', then it is the imperfect. (For which past tense to use, see Chapter 5.)

Formation

a) *-ar* verbs:
Remove *-ar* from infinitive, and add endings in *-aba*.

The Imperfect Tense

e.g. *escuch/ar*
*escuch**aba***   I was listening to, I used to listen to, I would listen to, I listened to
*escuch**abas***   etc.
*escuch**aba***
*escuch**ábamos***
*escuch**abais***
*escuch**aban***

b) *-er* and *-ir* verbs:
Remove *-er* or *-ir* from infinitive, and add endings in *-ía*.
e.g. *conoc/er*
*conoc**ía***   I used to know, I knew
*conoc**ías***   etc.
*conoc**ía***
*conoc**íamos***
*conoc**íais***
*conoc**ían***

Irregular Imperfects

ser, to be	*ir*, to go	*ver*, to see
era	iba	veía
eras	ibas	veías
era	iba	veía
éramos	íbamos	veíamos
erais	ibais	veíais
eran	iban	veían

● Other three-letter infinitives keep only the first letter in front of the endings.

     dar   *daba*   I was giving
     oír   *oía*   I was hearing

Use

a) Repeated actions in the past.
Le llamaba por teléfono cada dos horas pero nadie contestaba.
He telephoned him/her every two hours, but nobody answered.

b) Habit. Anything done regularly or always, or a habit or custom, needs the imperfect tense.
Cada verano iban de camping en Suiza.
Every summer they went ⎫
           used to go ⎬ camping in Switzerland.
           would go ⎭

c) Description. A state rather than an action needs the imperfect. Weather, descriptions of people's appearance or what they were wearing often fall into this category.

El sol brillaba y los pájaros cantaban en los árboles.
The sun was shining and the birds sang in the trees.

d) Background action. Any action that has been going on for an indefinite length of time when something else suddenly happens, needs the imperfect.

Me vestía cuando Ricardo llamó a la puerta.
I was getting dressed when Ricardo knocked at the door.

Warning signs

If any of the following is used, the imperfect may be needed:

cada día/mes/año	every day/month/year
los viernes	on Fridays
con frecuencia	often
cada vez que	whenever
siempre	always
a veces	sometimes
a menudo	often
de vez en cuando	from time to time

The Continuous Imperfect

Formation

The continuous imperfect is made up from the imperfect of *estar* + gerund.

estaba leyendo	I was reading
estabas durmiendo	you were sleeping
etc.	etc.

Use

For description, repeated or background action in the past (but not for a habit):

Charlaban en la plaza cuando el coche se paró.
They were chatting in the square when the car stopped.
(emphasises the car stopping)

Estaban charlando en la plaza cuando el coche se paró.
(emphasises what the people were doing when the car stopped)

Listening Practice

1. You are booking into a camp site with some friends. The owner tells you what the rules are.
    a) What must you do if you come back after 10 p.m.?
    b) What is forbidden beside the swimming-pool?
    c) Can you bring your dog?
    d) What is strictly forbidden, and why?

2. (Higher level) You're planning a picnic on the beach tomorrow, and decide to listen to the weather forecast.
    a) Should you go in the morning or the afternoon?
    b) Would it be better to go to the mountains instead?
    c) Will you need a jersey?

Answers:
1. (a) Leave your car in the car-park at the entrance to the site   (b) Washing your car   (c) No   (d) Lighting fires in the camp site; it could cause a fire and destroy a lot of tents.

2. (a) Afternoon (showers in morning)   (b) No – strong winds forecast   (c) No – temperature 25°.

Speaking Practice

1. You are touring Catalonia with a friend and want to book into a hotel in Barcelona for a few days. You begin:
    a) Ask if they have a room with two beds and a shower.
    Yes, for how long?
    b) Say it's for three nights.
    Do you want full board?
    c) Say you only want half board, please.
    Do you have an identity document?
    d) Tell him you have a passport; is that sufficient?

2. (Higher level) When you check out, you find there's a mistake in the bill. You begin.
    a) Tell the receptionist you think they've made a mistake.
    What is the problem?
    b) Say that there are 2 breakfasts on the bill and you didn't have breakfast.
    The price includes breakfast.
    c) Tell her the price-list ought to say this, but it doesn't.
    Would you like me to bring you the complaints book?
    d) Say 'yes, please', and you'd also like to speak to the manager.

7 A Chapter of Accidents

In this chapter you will revise talking about illness, injuries and accidents, going to the dentist and the chemist's. The grammar section revises comparisons, the perfect tense, and the imperative (orders).

A Headache

Sarah se despertó con un dolor de cabeza tremendo. Fue a buscar a la señora de Martínez.

—No me encuentro bien. No he dormido mucho, y me duele la cabeza.

—Pobrecita. ¿Tienes fiebre?

—No lo sé. Tengo frío y tengo ganas de vomitar.

—Bueno pues, oye, el padre de Elena tampoco ha dormido anoche. Tiene un dolor de muelas terrible. Acaba de pedir hora con el dentista, y para llegar al dentista tiene que pasar delante de la consulta del médico. Voy a telefonearle en seguida y Rafael te llevará en el coche antes de ir al dentista. A lo mejor tienes una pequeña insolación. Ayer pasaste demasiado tiempo al sol.

• • • • •

—¿Qué te ha dicho el médico?

—Tenía Vd. razón. Es una insolación. Tengo que guardar cama hasta mañana, y me ha recetado unas pastillas. No es nada grave.

—Menos mal. Me alegro mucho. Acuéstate ahora mismo y más tarde te subiré un té. Tienes que beber mucho, ¿no? Y mi marido, ¿dónde está?

—El dentista le ha puesto un empaste y dice que le duele mucho. Está en el comedor, con una copita de coñac.

—Lo necesitará. Javier acaba de telefonear desde Formigal. Se ha roto el tobillo. Tiene suerte; mucha gente se queda gravemente herida de un accidente de esquí. Y con las evaluaciones la semana que viene, una pierna rota sería el colmo. Además es el último día. Pero lo malo es que no puede viajar hasta pasado mañana.

Vocabulary

un dolor de cabeza headache	**vomitar** to be sick
no me encuentro bien I don't feel well	**un dolor de muelas** toothache
pobrecita poor thing	**pedir hora** to make an appointment
¿tienes fiebre? have you a temperature?	**la consulta** doctor's surgery
	a lo mejor perhaps

81

Describing Symptoms

> **una insolación** sunstroke, touch of the sun
> **guardar cama** to stay in bed
> **recetar** to prescribe
> **la pastilla** pill
> **no es nada grave** it's nothing serious
> **menos mal** thank goodness
> **te subiré un té** I'll bring you up a cup of tea
> **una copita de coñac** a glass of brandy
> **se ha roto el tobillo** he's broken his ankle
> **gravemente herido, -da** seriously injured
> **una pierna rota** a broken leg
> **es el colmo** it's the last straw
> **lo malo es que** the unfortunate thing is

Describing Symptoms

1. *Doler (ue)*, like *gustar* (Chapter 4), agrees with what hurts, and the person is indicated by the indefinite object pronoun. *Doler* is used only in the third person singular or plural.

me	duele	mucho	la garganta	my	throat	hurts	a lot
te		un poco	el hombro	your	shoulder		a bit
le		bastante	la muñeca	his, her, your	wrist		quite a bit
nos			el rodillo	our	knee		
os			el codo	your	elbow		
les			el pecho	their	chest		
	duelen		las piernas		legs	hurt	

2. *Tengo dolor de* + noun   I've got a ... ache.
   ¿Tienes dolor de estómago?   Have you got a stomach ache?
   Tenemos dolor de oído.   We've got earache.

At the Doctor's

> **tengo el cuello hinchado** I've got a swollen neck
> **toso mucho** I cough a lot
> **tienes tos** you've got a cough
> **tiene un resfriado** s/he's, you've got a cold
> **tenemos la gripe** we've got 'flu
> **están mareados** they're feeling sick, seasick
> **me he torcido el pie** I've twisted my foot
> **te has roto el dedo** you've broken your finger
> **se ha quemado la mano** s/he's, you've burnt your hand
> **¿puede Vd. recetarme algo?** can you give me a prescription?

First Aid

| le voy a recetar un jarabe I'm going to give you a prescription for cough syrup | ¿qué le debo? what do I owe you? |

At the Dentist's

| ¿puede Vd. darme hora hoy para el dentista? can you give me an appointment with the dentist today?
faltar a la cita to fail to keep an appointment | poner... to give...
...un empaste ...a filling
...una inyección ...an injection
hacer una radiografía to give an X-ray |

In the Chemist's

| la farmacia de guardia the chemist's on duty
¿tiene algo para... have you anything for...
...la indigestión? ...indigestion?
...las quemaduras del sol? ...sunburn?
...las picaduras de insecto? ...insect bites? | una caja de tiritas a box of sticking plasters
el esparadrapo sticking plaster
una bolsa de algodón a packet of cotton wool
vendar to bandage
le voy a poner una venda I'm going to bandage it for you |

- *La farmacia* sells medical items.
  La perfumería sells toiletries.
  La droguería sells household items, paint and toiletries, but NEVER medicines.

First Aid

PRIMEROS AUXILIOS

RECUERDE, Y SALVE VIDAS

—CONMOCION (CHOC): (piel pálida, fría; pulso cambiado); acostar, pies alzados. Aflojar ropa. Evitar que sude. Agua tibia (nada, si herida de vientre). Que hable.

—DESMAYO: Tender. Aflojar la ropa. Darle aire. Paños fríos.

—ELECTRICIDAD: Cortar la corriente; si no puede, apartarlo de ella con objeto, sin tocar con él su piel. RESPIRACION artificial.

—HERIDA de cuchillo, etc. No quitarlo (¡hemorragia!). Vendarlo también, sin presionarlo.

—QUEMADURA: acostar. No quitar la ropa adherida. Gasa o ropa en quemadura. Darle ánimos. No usar ungüentos. En incendios, envolver en telas y rodarlo por el suelo.

First Aid

Vocabulary

la conmoción shock	**el paño** cloth
aflojar loosen	**darle ánimos** comfort him/her
sudar to sweat	**los ungüentos** ointment
el vientre abdomen, stomach	**la tela** material, fabric
el desmayo faint	**rodar** to roll

Here is some good advice.

Muchos tipos de cáncer PUEDEN EVITARSE

1 - No fume.

2 - Modere el consumo de bebidas alcohólicas.

3 - Evita la exposición excesiva al sol.

4 - Siga las medidas de higiene, protección y seguridad en el trabajo.

5 - Coma frecuentemente frutas y verduras frescas.

6 - Evite el exceso de peso.

Accidents

la contusión bruise	el puesto de primeros
el rasguño scratch	auxilios first-aid post
la herida injury	Urgencias Casualty Department
¿está herido, -da? are you hurt?	¿tiene su póliza de seguro? have
la piel skin	you got your insurance policy?
¿puede llamar una ambulancia,	la camilla stretcher
por favor? please, will you call	la silla de ruedas wheelchair
an ambulance?	tengo el brazo escayolado I've
la cruz roja española Spanish	got my arm in plaster
Red Cross	

Comparisons
More, Less (Comparatives)

		Adjective	Adverb
more más more ... than más ... que		Mi conejo es más bonito. My rabbit is prettier. Los caballos son más grandes que los burros. Horses are bigger than donkeys.	Rosa corre más rápidamente. Rosa runs faster. Un gato aprende más despacio que un perro. A cat learns more slowly than a dog.
less menos less ... than menos ... que		Este libro es menos interesante. This book is less interesting. El latín es menos difícil que el griego. Latin is less difficult than Greek.	El brazo me duele menos que la pierna. My arm hurts less than my leg. Ahora escribe menos alegremente. Now he writes less cheerfully.
as ... as tan ... como		Eva es tan alta como yo. Eva is as tall as I am. Las notas no son tan importantes como aprobar los exámenes. The grades are not as important as passing the exams.	Julio no trabaja tan cuidadosamente como su padre. Julio doesn't work as carefully as his father.

Comparisons

The Most, the Least (Superlatives)

	Adjective	Adverb
the most *el más* *la más* *los más* *las más*	*Este libro es el más interesante.* This book is the most interesting. *Esa casa es la más bonita.* That house is the prettiest. *Estos zapatos son los más caros.* These shoes are the dearest. *Aquellas faldas son las más feas.* Those skirts are the ugliest.	Same as comparative: *Andrés trabaja más cuidadosamente.* Andrés works . . . . . . more carefully . . . the most carefully.
the least *el menos* *la menos* *los menos* *las menos*	*Ese perro es el menos obediente.* That dog is the least obedient. *Esta película es la menos aburrida.* This film is the least boring. *Esos melones son los menos frescos.* Those melons are the least fresh. *Estas galletas son las menos dulces.* These biscuits are the least sweet.	Same as comparative: *Victoria escribe menos rápidamente.* Victoria writes . . . . . . less quickly . . . the least quickly.

- *Esta película es más interesante.* This film is more interesting.
  Esta película es la más interesante. This film is the most interesting.

But: *La película más interesante* The more interesting film
  The most interesting film

86

NOT *La película la más interesante*; the article *el*, *la*, *los*, *las* is omitted AFTER A NOUN.

Irregular Comparatives and Superlatives

Adjective	Comparative	Superlative	Adverb	Comparative & Superlative
bueno,-na good	*mejor(es)* better	*el/la mejor* *los/las mejores* the best	*bien* well	*mejor* better, best
malo,-la bad	*peor(es)*	*el/la peor* *los/las peores* the worst	*mal* badly	*peor* worse, the worst
grande big, great	*más grande(s)* bigger *mayor(es)* older, greater	*el/la más grande* *los/las más grandes* the biggest *el/la mayor* *los/las mayores* the oldest, the greatest	*mucho* a lot	*más* more, most
pequeño,-ña small	*más pequeño,-ña* smaller *menor(es)* younger, less	*el/la más pequeño,-ña* *los/las más pequeños, pequeñas* the smallest *el/la menor* *los/las menores* the youngest, the least	*poco* a little	*menos* less, the least

Aquellas niñas son las más grandes, pero son las menores de la clase.
Those girls are the biggest, but they're the youngest in the class.
Es el mejor portero del mundo, pero ayer jugó tan mal que pareció el peor. He's the best goalkeeper in the world, but he played so badly yesterday he seemed like the worst.

87

The Perfect Tense

- Adjectives agree with the noun they describe; adverbs NEVER change.
    - e.g. *Las chicas son mejores*. (adjective) The girls are better.
    Las chicas cantan mejor. (adverb) The girls sing better/the best.

- 'In' after a superlative is *de* in Spanish.
    - e.g. *Las montañas más altas de los Pirineos*. The highest mountains in the Pyrenees.

The Perfect Tense

The perfect tense is used for events that have happened very recently. The normal past tense is the preterite. The English equivalent is 'I have asked'.

e.g. *¿Qué has hecho hoy?* What have you done/did you do today?
He visitado el museo del Prado. I've been/I went to the Prado art gallery.

But: *Oye, ¿has visto los sellos que compré anteayer?* I say, have you seen the stamps I bought the day before yesterday?
(*has visto* – perfect; *compré* – preterite)

Oye, ¿has visto los sellos que compré anteayer?

Formation

There are two words in the perfect tense. *Haber* is used for 'have' (NOT *tener*); and the past participle is formed by removing -*ar*, -*er* or -*ir* from the infinitive and adding -*ado* to -*ar* verbs and -*ido* to -*er* and -*ir* verbs.

The Perfect Tense

Present tense of *haber*	Past participle	
he has ha hemos habéis han	*hablado* ⎱ -*ar* verbs *comprado* ⎰ *vendido* ⎱ -*er* verbs *comido* ⎰ *vivido* ⎱ -*ir* verbs *recibido* ⎰	I have spoken you have bought s/he, you(*Vd.*) has/have sold we have eaten, had lunch you have lived they, you (*Vds.*) have received

Use

a) The past participle <u>never agrees</u> when used with *haber*.
   e.g. *Las niñas <u>han llegado</u>.*   The little girls have arrived.
   Los <u>hemos encontrado</u> en la calle.   We met them in the street.

   It does agree when not used with *haber*.
   e.g. *La puerta está cerrada.*   The door is closed.

b) The two parts of the perfect tense are <u>never separated</u>.
   e.g. *¿<u>Ha comprado</u> Vd. la casa?*   <u>Have</u> you <u>bought</u> the house?
   <u>He pensado</u> siempre que es ridículo.   I <u>have</u> always <u>thought</u> it's ridiculous.

c) Reflexive and object pronouns go before *haber*.
   e.g. *Me lo <u>ha dicho</u> muchas veces.*   He's often told me so.
   Se <u>han acostado</u>.   They've gone to bed.

Irregular Past Participles

Infinitive	Perfect Tense	
abrir	*he abierto*	I have opened
cubrir	*has cubierto*	you have covered
descubrir	*ha descubierto*	s/he, you (*Vd.*) has/have discovered
decir	*hemos dicho*	we have said
hacer	*habéis hecho*	you have done/made
morir	*han muerto*	they, you *(Vds.)* have died
escribir	*he escrito*	I have written
poner	*has puesto*	you have put
romper	*ha roto*	s/he, you(*Vd.*) has/have broken
ver	*hemos visto*	we have seen
volver	*habéis vuelto*	you have returned

The Imperative

The imperative is used to give orders. Avoid by using *quiere(s)* + infinitive (see page 111).

Affirmative			Negative	
tú	3rd person singular present tense		*no* + present subjunctive	
cantar	*¡canta!*	sing!	*¡no cantes!*	don't sing!
beber	*¡bebe!*	drink!	*¡no bebas!*	don't drink!
escribir	*¡escribe!*	write!	*¡no escribas!*	don't write!
Vd., Vds.	present subjunctive		*no* + affirmative	
pensar	*¡piense!* *¡piensen!*	think!	*¡no piense!* *¡no piensen!*	don't think!
mover	*¡mueva!* *¡muevan!*	move!	*¡no mueva!* *¡no muevan!*	don't move!
pedir	*¡pida!* *¡pidan!*	ask!	*¡no pida!* *¡no pidan!*	don't ask!
vosotros	remove *r* from infinitive, add *d* (all verbs)		*no* + present subjunctive	
estar	*¡estad!*	be!	*¡no estéis!*	don't be!
ver	*¡ved!*	see!	*¡no veáis!*	don't see!
compartir	*¡compartid!*	share!	*¡no compartáis!*	don't share!

Irregular Imperatives

	Affirmative		Negative		
	tú	*Vd.,Vds.*	*tú*	*Vd.,Vds.*	
decir	*¡di!*	*¡diga(n) Vd(s).!* speak!	*¡no digas!*	*¡no diga(n)!*	don't say!
hacer	*¡haz!*	*¡haga(n) Vd(s).!* do!	*¡no hagas!*	(*no* + affirmative)	don't do!
ir	*¡ve!*	*¡vaya(n) Vd(s).!* go!	*¡no vayas!*		don't go!
poner	*¡pon!*	*¡ponga(n) Vd(s).!* put!	*¡no pongas!*		don't put!
salir	*¡sal!*	*¡salga(n) Vd(s).!* leave!	*¡no salgas!*		don't leave!
ser	*¡sé!*	*¡sea(n) Vd(s).!* be!	*¡no seas!*		don't be!
tener	*¡ten!*	*¡tenga(n) Vd(s).!* have!	*¡no tengas!*		don't have!
venir	*¡ven!*	*¡venga(n) Vd(s).!* come!	*¡no vengas!*		don't come!

Reflexive Verbs

Affirmative (Pronouns attached to end of verb)		Negative (Pronouns in front of verb)	
tú	¡levántate! get up!	¡no te levantes!	don't get up!
Vd.	¡levántese!	¡no se levante!	
Vds.	¡siéntense! sit down!	¡no se sienten!	don't sit down!
vosotros	¡sentaos! (NOT sentados; d is dropped before -os. Exception: idos, go away)	¡no os sentéis!	

¡No se siente!

- Object Pronouns with imperative go in same position as reflexive pronouns above.

Listening Practice

1. Listening to the radio one night, you hear this item about an accident.
    a) What time did the accident happen?
    b) What vehicles were involved?
    c) How did the accident happen?
    d) What happened to the people involved?

2. (Higher level) You feel ill while on holiday in Spain, and go to the doctor. In case you forget, you write down briefly in English what he tells you.
    a) What are you to do first?
    b) When must you take the pills?
    c) What else is prescribed?
    d) What must you not do?
    e) What are you to eat and drink?
    f) What if you don't feel any better?

Answers:
1. (a) 6 p.m. (b) A car and a motor-cycle (c) The car was passing a parked lorry when the motor-cyclist came out of a street in front of it (d) The car driver was injured, but the motor-cyclist only had bruises.

2. (a) Take the prescription to the chemist's (b) Three times a day, after meals (c) Cough syrup (d) Swim or sunbathe (for a few days) (e) Mineral water; eat what you like (f) Come back after a week.

Speaking Practice

1. You feel ill while staying with your Spanish friend. The doctor comes to see you:
    Good morning. What's the matter with you?
- a) Tell the doctor you have a headache, and you think you've got a temperature.
Have you been sick?
- b) Say yes, three or four times during the night.
I think you've eaten something that doesn't agree with you.
- c) Ask if he can prescribe something for you.
Yes, I'll give you some tablets.
- d) Ask if you have to stay in bed.
No, but you mustn't eat anything for 24 hours.

2. (Higher level) This is a more difficult open-ended question.
While on holiday in Spain you wake up with a dreadful toothache. Phone the dentist and ask if you can make an appointment. You are in pain, so obviously you want one as soon as possible. Continue the conversation until an appointment is made.

<u>Remember</u>, you have agreed to meet an old friend of your parents for lunch tomorrow at 1 p.m., and you don't know how to get in touch with him.

The dentist's receptionist answers the telephone and begins . . .

(In this role-play, the responses on the tape are only suggested replies. Your own answers may be just as good. The important thing is to practise this type of question.)

8 Using Public Services

This chapter will help you to talk about using the bank, the post office and the telephone and describing lost property. There are useful phrases for getting things done, and the grammar section revises pronouns, how to translate 'can' and 'know', which tense to use for emotions, and the pluperfect tense.

Going to the Bank

Sarah decidió ir de compras sola, dejando en casa a Elena, que quería repasar sus apuntes. Cogió el autobús hasta el centro, bajó y se dirigió hacia un banco. Tuvo que hacer cola, pero al fin llegó a la ventanilla.

—Buenos días. Quisiera cambiar cheques de viaje por un valor de veinte libras esterlinas. ¿Los firmo ahora?

—Sí. ¿Me deja su pasaporte, por favor?

—Aquí tiene. Tengo también un billete de diez libras. ¿Me lo puede cambiar?

—Claro que sí. Firme aquí. Tenga su pasaporte. Su número es el sesenta y dos. Cuando llamen su número, pase por caja.

Vocabulary

repasar los apuntes to revise notes
bajar (de) to get off (bus, train)
dirigirse hacia to make one's way to
hacer cola to queue
el cheque de viaje traveller's cheque
por un valor de for the sum of
¿los firmo ahora? shall I sign them now?
¿me deja su pasaporte? may I have your passport?
un billete de diez libras a ten-pound note
¿me lo puede cambiar? can you change it for me?
firme aquí sign here
cuando llamen su número, pase por caja when they call your number, go to the cashier

Useful Vocabulary

¿se puede cambiar moneda extranjera? can one change foreign money?
¿cuánto vale la libra esterlina hoy? what is the exchange rate for the pound today?
cobrar un cheque to cash a cheque
el talonario cheque-book
el mostrador counter
los ahorros savings
un duro 5 pesetas

93

In the Post Office

Luego Sarah fue a correos.
—Quiero mandar este paquete a Inglaterra.
—Muy bien. Tiene que rellenar una etiqueta verde para la aduana. ¿Quiere enviarlo certificado?
—No, gracias. ¿Cuánto cuesta?
—Depende del peso. Y si quiere enviarlo por avión, es más caro.
—¿Cuánto tardará en llegar si no lo mando por avión?
—De dos a tres semanas más.
—Lo mando por avión entonces. Quisiera también enviar un telegrama a Inglaterra.
—Necesita Vd. este formulario.
—Y una postal a Inglaterra, ¿cuánto es?
—Cuarenta y cinco pesetas. Igual que una carta.
—Pues déme tres sellos de cuarenta y cinco pesetas por favor. Tengo que enviar una carta urgente, pero es para España. ¿Cuánto cuesta?
—Noventa pesetas.

Vocabulary

quiero mandar este paquete a Inglaterra I want to send this parcel to England	**¿quiere enviarlo certificado?** do you want to send it by registered post?
rellenar una etiqueta verde para la aduana to fill in a Green Label for the Customs	**¿cuánto tardará en llegar?** how long will it take to arrive?
el peso weight	**de dos a tres semanas más** from two to three weeks more
el formulario form	

Lost and Found

Al dejar correos, Sarah se dio cuenta de repente de que había dejado su bolso en el banco. Sólo tenía el monedero que llevaba en el bolsillo. ¿Qué hacer? No tenía tiempo de volver al banco porque cerraba a los dos. Tendría que llamar por teléfono. Sarah preguntó a un transeúnte si había una cabina telefónica por allí. El senor le contestó que debería ir a la telefónica, que estaba muy cerca. Sarah fue corriendo a la telefónica, buscó el número del banco en la guía de teléfonos, y marcó el número. Poco después un empleado le contestó – y le dijo que habían llevado su bolso a la oficina de objetos perdidos. Llegada a la oficina, Sarah describió el bolso y se lo entregaron con todo el contenido sano y salvo. ¡Qué suerte!

Vocabulary

darse cuenta de to realise	**marcar el número** to dial the number
el monedero purse	**poco después** soon
el bolsillo pocket	**un empleado** employee
¿qué hacer? what was to be done?	**la oficina de objetos perdidos** lost-property office
un transeúnte a passer-by	**entregar** to hand over
una cabina telefónica public call-box	**sano y salvo** safe and sound
la telefónica telephone exchange	**¡qué suerte!** what luck!
la guía de teléfonos telephone directory	

Useful Words and Phrases

Telephone Vocabulary

un locutorio phone booth	**nos han cortado** we were cut off
el prefijo dialling code	**se ha equivocado de número** you've got the wrong number
espere la señal para marcar wait for the dialling tone	**dígame** hello (on telephone)
la conferencia long-distance call	**no se retire** hold the line
una conferencia de cobro revertido reverse charge call	**al habla** } speaking **al aparato** }
descolgar (ue) el microteléfono to lift the receiver	**¿puede ponerme con ...?** may I speak to ...?
colgar (ue) to hang up	**¿de parte de quién?** who's speaking?
el auricular receiver	**de parte del señor Ortiz** Mr. Ortiz speaking
no contesta no reply	
está comunicando it's engaged	

Getting Things Done

¿puede Vd. ... could you ...	**la comisaría** police station
... plancharme esta camisa? ... iron this shirt for me?	**quiero denunciar un robo** I want to report a theft
... limpiarme este pantalón? ... clean these trousers?	**revelar** to develop (film)
... quitar esta mancha de la falda? ... get this stain off my skirt?	**¿para diapositivas o para papel?** for slides or prints?
... arreglar el televisor? ... mend the television set?	**¿quiere Vd. ...** will you ...
la tintorería the dry-cleaner's	**... cortarme el pelo?** ... cut my hair?
limpiar en seco to dry-clean	**... mandarlo a casa?** ... send it to the house?

Lost Property

To describe something you have lost or found, you should include the following information.

1. <u>What</u> is it?

He perdido	I've lost	mi	cartera	my	wallet, briefcase
Me han robado	Someone's stolen		billetero		wallet
He encontrado	I've found	una	sortija	a	ring
			pulsera		bracelet
			cadena		chain
	un	collar		necklace

2. <u>Where</u> did you lose/find it?
    Lo/la he dejado en el autobús. I left it in the bus.
    Estaba en el supermercado cuando lo/la encontré. I was in the supermarket when I found it.
    Estaba en el parque de atracciones cuando me lo/la robaron. I was in the fun-fair when it was stolen.

3. <u>When</u> was it lost/found?
    ... el sábado por la noche ... on Saturday night

4. <u>What's it like?</u>
    ¿Dé qué tamaño es? What size is it?
    Colour: *Es gris oscuro.* It's dark grey.
            Es verde claro. It's light green.
    Made of: *Es de cuero.* It's leather.
            ... de oro ... gold
            ... de plata ... silver
            ... de perlas ... pearl
    Old/new: *viejo, antiguo, nuevo*
    Value: *Es de mucho valor.* It's very valuable.

5. <u>What make</u> (*la marca*) is it?
    Es una Kodak.
    Es un Renault. *la matrícula* registration number

6. <u>What's inside it?</u>
    Contenía los billetes de avión. It had the plane tickets in it.
        ... unas fotos de mi familia. ... family photos....
        ... mi agenda. ... my diary....

7. Make sure you can do the following.
   a) Spell your name and address.
   b) Give your telephone number (in pairs of numbers, so 425701 is *el cuarenta y dos, cincuenta y siete, cero, uno*).
   c) End the conversation.
      Quisiera saber si alguien lo ha encontrado.   I'd like to know if it's been found.
      ¿Me avisará si se lo entrega?   Will you let me know if it's handed in?

Pronouns
1. Subject Pronouns

yo	I	*nosotros/nosotras*	we (m. and f.)
tú	you (sing. familiar)	*vosotros/vosotras*	you (pl. familiar, m. and f.)
él	he	*ellos*	they (m.)
ella	she	*ellas*	they (f.)
Vd.	you (sing. polite)	*Vds.*	you (pl. polite)

a) If a subject pronoun (except *Vd.*) is used, it is emphasised.
   e.g. <u>*Yo*</u> *hablo ruso, chino y japonés, pero* <u>*él*</u> *sólo habla inglés*.
   <u>I</u> speak Russian, Chinese and Japanese, but <u>he</u> only speaks English.

b) Subject pronouns may be used to avoid confusion.
   e.g. *Mientras hablaba, escuchaba* is not clear and could mean 'I, s/he or you were speaking, listening,' or both.
   But in *Mientras* <u>*ella*</u> *hablaba,* <u>*yo*</u> *escuchaba*, it is clear she was talking and I was listening.

c) Subject pronouns are used after *ser*, and the verb agrees with the pronoun.
   e.g. <u>*Soy*</u> *yo*. It's me.   <u>*Somos*</u> *nosotros*. It's us.

d) The neuter pronoun *ello* is used ONLY when there is no noun it can refer to.
   e.g. *Antonio dice que no sabe nada de* <u>*ello*</u>.
      Antonio says he knows nothing about <u>it</u>.
      (The 'it' is something like 'how the vase got broken', not a noun like 'the letter'.)

2. Disjunctive (Strong) Pronouns

Used after a preposition (*de, a, para, por, sin, en*, etc.)

mí	me	nosotros/nosotras	us (m. and f.)
ti	you (sing. familiar)	vosotros/vosotras	you (pl. familiar, m. and f.)
él	he	ellos	them (m.)
ella	she	ellas	them (f.)
Vd.	you (sing. polite)	Vds.	you (pl. polite)

    e.g. *Estoy pensando en vosotros.* I'm thinking of you.
        Cada noche soñaba con ella. Every night he used to dream of her.

- Note the special forms with *con*:
  conmigo   with me
  contigo   with you
  consigo   with himself/herself/themselves/yourself/yourselves

But: *con él, con nosotros, para mí, de ti*, etc.

- There is a reflexive form *sí* for the third person singular and plural, used when the pronoun refers back to the subject of the verb.
  e.g. *Compró la casa para sí.* He bought the house for himself. (same person)
  Compró la casa para él. He (one person) bought the house for him. (another person)

3. Object Pronouns

Direct Object		Indirect Object		Direct and Indirect the Same	
lo (m.sing. thing)	it	*le*	to him, to her, to you (*Vd.*)	*me*	me, to me
lo, le (m.sing. person)	him, you (*Vd.*)			*te*	you, to you (sing. familiar)
la (f.sing. thing or person)	it, her, you (*Vd.*)	*les*	to them (m. and f.), to you (*Vds.*)	*nos*	us, to us
los (m.pl. thing or person)	them, you (*Vds.*)			*os*	you, to you (pl. familiar)
las (f. pl. thing or person)	them, you (*Vds.*)				

Pronouns

- Third person direct object pronouns (except m. singular *lo*, *le*) are the same as the word for 'the'.
  e.g. *Comieron las uvas.* They ate the grapes.
  Las comieron. They ate them.

- Masculine singular *lo* is for things, *lo* or *le* for people. *La* is for both things and people.
  e.g. *Lo vimos* ⎫   We saw it   ⎫
       Lo/le vimos ⎬ *en Cádiz.*   him   ⎬ in Cadiz.
       La vimos   ⎭   it/her   ⎭

4. Position of Object Pronouns

These come before the verb, not after as in English.
  e.g. *No te oigo bien.* I can't hear you very well.

No te oigo bien.

ALWAYS put indirect first, then direct object.
  e.g. *Os lo hemos dicho.* We told you so.
  Me las dio en seguida. He gave me them at once.

BUT pronoun objects come AFTER the verb, written as one word, when the verb is an infinitive, a gerund, or an affirmative imperative.

a) Infinitive.
  e.g. *Tenemos que comprártela.* We'll have to buy you it.
  Mezclarlo bien antes de ponerlo al horno. Mix it well before putting it in the oven.

b) Gerund.
  e.g. *Cogiéndola por la mano, se puso a correr.* Seizing her by the hand, he began to run.
  Está preparándonoslos. He's preparing them for us.

- When there is another verb directly before the gerund or infinitive, pronoun objects can be placed in front of this first verb.
  e.g. *Te la tenemos que comprar.* We'll have to buy you it.
  Nos los está preparando. He's preparing them for us.

99

c) Affirmative imperative.
   e.g. *Abrelo en seguida*.   Open it at once.

But: Pronoun objects go before a negative imperative.
   e.g. *No lo abras*.   Don't open it.

5. Two Third-Person Pronoun Objects

The indirect object (*le* or *les*) becomes *se* when followed by *lo*, *la*, *los* or *las*. *Se* can mean 'to him', 'to her', 'to you', (*Vd.* or *Vds.*) or 'to them'.
   e.g. *Se* (to him) *las (las manzanas) mandé*.   I sent him (indirect object) them (direct object).
   It could also mean 'I sent her, you or them them'.

• Do not confuse *se* the indirect object with *se* the third person reflexive pronoun (*se acostó*, he went to bed). The indirect object *se* is ALWAYS followed by a third-person direct object pronoun (*lo, la, los* or *las*).

'Poder/Saber/Conocer': Can and Know

Poder	Saber	Conocer
a) To be physically able to: *No puede jugar en el partido; se ha roto el pulgar.* He can't play in the match; he's broken his thumb.	a) To know how to: *¿Sabes nadar?* Can you swim?	a) To know a person: *¿Conoces a Carmen?* Do you know Carmen? But in preterite = 'to meet for first time': *En Palma conocimos a unos suecos muy simpáticos.* In Palma we met some very nice Swedes.
b) Asking permission: *¿Puedo dejar un recado?* May I leave a message?	b) To know a fact: *Todo el mundo sabe que Madrid es la capital de España.* Everybody knows Madrid is the capital of Spain.	b) To know a place: *Yo no conozco este barrio: estamos perdidos.* I don't know this part of town; we're lost.

¿Sabes nadar?

Which Tense with Emotions?

Preterite

Is there a particular moment at which the person began to feel sad, angry, etc.? If so, use the preterite.

Cuando el policía le devolvió su monedero, estuvo muy contenta.
When the policeman gave her back her purse, she was very happy.
(i.e. she began to feel happy at the moment when he gave it back)

If you could say 'became' instead of 'was', use the preterite. *Ponerse* is often better Spanish.

El señor se puso enfadado al oír que alguien le había robado el coche.
The man was angry when he heard someone had stolen his car.

Imperfect

Use the imperfect to describe someone's state of mind over an indefinite period.

Rocío estaba muy triste en Granada. Echaba de menos a sus amigos en Sevilla.
Rocío was very unhappy in Granada. She missed her friends in Seville.

'Querer/Saber/Poder': Wanting, Knowing or Being Able To

Wanting, knowing or being able to do something: these rarely refer to a particular moment. Use the imperfect unless you have a good reason to use the preterite.

    e.g. *No quería volver a Inglaterra.* I didn't want to go back to England.

    But: *No quise volver a Inglaterra* (preterite) means 'I refused to go back to England', because it happened at one precise moment.

101

¿*Pero no sabías su nombre?* But didn't you know his name?
But: *El miércoles supe su nombre* (preterite) means 'On Wednesday I learnt his name'. *Saber* used in the preterite means 'to find out, get to know'.

The Pluperfect Tense
Formation
It has two parts – the imperfect of *haber* + past participle. The same rules apply as in the perfect tense (see Chapter 7).

había hablado	} -ar verbs	I had spoken
habías comprado		you had bought
había comido	} -er verbs	s/he, you (*Vd.*) had eaten
habíamos bebido		we had drunk
habíais vivido	} -ir verbs	you had lived
habían repetido		they, you (*Vds.*), had repeated

Use
The pluperfect is used for an action in the past that was completed before the action of the main verb in the sentence took place.
    e.g. *Perdimos el tren porque no habíamos oído el despertador.*
        We missed the train because we hadn't heard the alarm clock.
        (Not hearing the alarm is over before missing the train.)

- DO NOT USE
The pluperfect must not be used when
    a) the main verb is in the preterite
       AND
    b) the second verb is introduced by *cuando* (when), *en cuanto* (as soon as), *apenas* (scarcely, hardly).

If both the above apply, use the preterite for both verbs.
    e.g. *Cuando terminó, salió.*
        When he had finished, he left.
        Me eché a llorar en cuanto leí la carta.
        I burst into tears as soon as I had read the letter.
        Apenas llegamos cuando sonó el timbre.
        We had scarcely arrived when the bell rang.

Listening Practice

1. You are on a day trip to Tangier. On the boat you hear this announcement over the loudspeaker.

a) What has been found?
b) Describe it.
d) What must you do if it's yours?

2. (Higher level) In a programme about the new season's offerings on Spanish television you hear this item about a series returning to the screen.
   a) What channel will the series be shown on?
   b) Why have they changed the time of the programme?
   c) Several new episodes have been filmed. What is different about the setting of these episodes?
   d) What is suggested may happen as a result of showing these programmes?

Answers:
1. (a) A watch (b) It's gold, with the initials FMS (c) Go to the office next to the restaurant.
2. (a) Channel 2 (b) To ensure a wide audience (c) The first series was set in the American West; the new series is filmed in China (d) A revival of interest in the martial arts (karate and judo are specifically mentioned).

Speaking Practice

1. You have lost your younger brother while at the fun-fair and have gone to the Lost Children's Room to see if he has been found. You begin.
   a) Tell the lady in charge that you've lost your younger brother in the fun-fair.
      How old is he?
   b) Tell her he's seven.
      What does he look like?
   c) Say that he's blond, with blue eyes.
      What is he wearing?
   d) Red trousers and a white shirt, with red socks and sandals.

2. (Higher level)
Situation: You are travelling from Barcelona to Valencia by train. You discover you have lost your wallet, which contains your train ticket and all your money. A ticket inspector comes into your carriage.
You must:
   a) Explain the problem.
   b) Tell the inspector where you got on the train and where you're travelling to.
   c) Continue the conversation until the problem is solved.

9 A Shopping Trip

This chapter deals with shopping, returning purchases, making a formal complaint and describing a disastrous holiday. There is advice on writing messages, telling someone to do something, and on making yourself understood. The grammar section revises 'lo' with an adjective or an adverb, the conditional tense and 'if' clauses.

Buying Presents

La visita de Sarah toca a su fin. Ya se siente una más de la familia, comprende casi todo lo que se le dice, puede hacerse comprender, se ha hecho nuevas amistades y le gusta mucho el estilo de vida en Sevilla. Sin embargo, tiene que volver a casa el fin de semana que viene, y sale de compras por última vez en busca de regalos para sus padres y hermanos. Elena la acompaña porque quiere cambiar una camiseta que acaba de comprar. Entran en el almacén y van a la sección de regalos.

—Buenos días. ¿Qué desean?
—Busco regalos para mis padres. Quisiera algo típico de España. Había pensado en algo de cerámica para mi madre.
—¿Le gusta este plato con la bailaora flamenca?
—No, realmente no. Los colores son muy chillones. No le gustaría.

¿Qué le parece este jarro verde?

—¿Qué le parece este jarro verde? Es cerámica de la Cartuja, ¿sabe?, que se fabrica aquí en Sevilla.
—Sí, es muy bonito, pero es demasiado grande. ¿No tiene nada más barato?
—A ver. Este cenicero no es caro. O tenemos azulejos con escenas de la feria de abril.
—Me quedo con el cenicero. Será ideal para mi padre.

—¿Se lo envuelvo?
—Sí, por favor. ¿Pago aquí?
—No. Pase Vd. a la caja, por aquí.

Vocabulary

tocar a su fin   to draw to an end
ya se siente una más de la familia
   she feels like one of the family now
comprende casi todo lo que se le dice   she understands nearly everything that's said to her
puede hacerse comprender   she can make herself understood
se ha hecho nuevas amistades
   she's made new friends
el estilo de vida   way of life
por última vez   for the last time
sale de compras   she goes out shopping
en busca de   in search of
el almacén   department store
la sección de regalos   gift department
la cerámica   pottery
la bailaora flamenca   flamenco dancer
los colores son muy chillones
   the colours are very loud
el jarro   jug
cerámica de la Cartuja   typical china from Seville.
¿no tiene nada más barato?
   haven't you anything cheaper?
el cenicero   ashtray
el azulejo   tile
la feria de abril   April Fair in Seville
¿se lo envuelvo?   shall I wrap it for you?

Returning a Purchase

En la sección de modas, Elena habla con la dependienta.
—Señora, compré esta camiseta hace dos días, y al llegar a casa vi que había una mancha en la espalda. ¿Me la puede cambiar?
—¿Tiene Vd. el recibo?
—Aquí lo tiene.
—Y ¿ es de qué talla?
—Cuarenta.
—Vamos a ver. ¿Le importa el color?
—Sí, claro. La compré porque el color va bien con esta falda.
—Lo siento. Sólo tenemos esta talla en rosa, verde oscuro o azul marino. No quedan en azul claro.
—Entonces tendrá que devolverme el dinero.

Vocabulary

la sección de modas   fashion department
¿le importa el color?   does the colour matter?

Useful Words and Phrases

la dependienta shop assistant	**el color va bien con ...** the colour goes well with ...
una mancha en la espalda a mark on the back	**– ¿de qué talla?** what size?
¿me la puede cambiar? can you change it for me?	**– cuarenta** size 12
el recibo receipt	**tendrá que devolverme el dinero** you will have to give me my money back
azul marino navy blue	

Useful Words and Phrases

You need to be able to ask for what you want, for something different, to be able to say why something is not suitable. You must be able to understand what the shop assistant says to you as well.

Shopping Vocabulary

¿en qué puedo servirle? can I help you?
¿algo más? ⎱
¿alguna cosa más? ⎬ anything else?
¿es todo? ⎰
las rebajas sales
la rebaja reduction
la promoción special offer
la liquidación clearance sale
la ganga bargain
a mitad del precio half price
¿es para ... is it for ...
　... regalar? ... a present?
　... una persona mayor? ... an older person?
¿cómo paga, en metálico? how are you paying, in cash?
pague en caja pay at the cash desk
entrega a domicilio we deliver

envío gratuito a domicilio free delivery
ir de tiendas to go shopping
hay uno/una en el escaparate there's one in the window
¿me puede enseñar otro/otra? can you show me another?
no puedo gastar tanto I can't afford it
¿puede enseñarme otro más pequeño? can you show me a smaller one?
la sección hogar household goods department
la sección recreativos sport, toys, TV dept
la sección complementos accessories

Vocabulary: Clothes

la tienda de confecciones clothes shop
la sastrería tailor's
¿sabe la medida? do you know the measurements?

se puede lavar a mano hand washable
no encoge won't shrink
¿se lo puedo probar? may I try it on?

Useful Words and Phrases

Spanish	English	Spanish	English
¿qué número calza? ¿qué número gasta?	what size shoe do you take?	son un poco estrechos	they're a bit tight
¿con manga corta o larga?	short or long sleeves?	¿lo tiene en . . . . . . azul?	do you have it in . . . . . . blue?
¿quiere probárselo?	do you want to try it on?	. . . algodón? . . . lana?	. . . cotton? . . . wool?
le va muy bien le cae muy bien	it really suits you	es muy . . . . . . largo	it's very . . . . . . long
le van mejor, ¿no?	those are better, aren't they?	. . . corto . . . cómodo	. . . short . . . comfortable
la cremallera	zip	me parece	I think it's
no quedan de ese . . . . . . modelo	there are none left in that . . . . . . model	muy . . . . . . bonito . . . caro	very . . . . . . pretty . . . dear
. . . número	. . . shoe size	está de moda	it's in fashion
no quedan de esa talla	there are none left in that size	está pasado de moda	it's out of date, unfashionable
se puede lavar a máquina	machine washable		

Food

Remember:

- Quantities and containers are ALWAYS followed by *de*.
- *Medio*, *media* is <u>never</u> used with *un* or *una*.

Asking for . . .	Quantities		
póngame, give me (for things, needing to be measured; e.g. petrol, potatoes) *déme*, give me *quisiera*, I'd like	*un litro de*	*leche fresca*	a litre of fresh milk
	medio kilo de	*manzanas*	half a kilo of apples
	cien gramos de	*mantequilla*	100 grams of butter
	un sobre de	*aspirinas*	a packet of aspirins
	una botella de	*gaseosa*	a bottle of fizzy lemonade
	un frasco de	*perfume*	a bottle of perfume
	un paquete de	*arroz*	a packet of rice
	una caja de	*cerillas*	a box of matches
	una lata de	*guisantes*	a tin of peas
	un trozo de	*jamón*	a slice of ham
	una barra de	*pan*	a loaf of bread

Vocabulary: Food

sólo tenemos botellas de medio litro we only have half-litre bottles
vino tinto no queda there's no red wine left
se han acabado las zanahorias the carrots are finished
son fresquísimos, -mas they're really fresh

¿le doy una bolsa de plástico? would you like a plastic (carrier) bag?
los melocotones no llegarán hasta mañana the peaches won't arrive until tomorrow

Vocabulary: Gifts

el recuerdo souvenir
el llavero key-ring
el abanico fan
la muñeca doll
las castañuelas castanets
los pendientes ear-rings
la bisutería costume jewellery
el florero vase

¿los/las puede cambiar si no le gustan? can s/he change them if s/he doesn't like them?
guarde el recibo keep the receipt
me lo envuelve para regalo por favor will you gift-wrap it, please

Vocabulary: Other Shops

la mantequería dairy
la confitería sweet-shop
los bombones chocolates
el chicle chewing-gum
la pastelería cake shop
la tarta large fancy cake
el bizcocho sponge cake
el polo ice lolly

el barquillo cornet
la tienda de comestibles } food shop, grocer's
la tienda de ultramarinos }
la tienda de calzado shoe shop
la papelería stationer's
la librería bookshop

Complaints

1. Formal: To a Business

You may be asked to complain to a travel agent, a car-hire company or a shop. For a written complaint, see the formal letter on page 52.

puede Vd. arreglarlo/la	can you mend it
cambiarlo/la	change it
sustituirlo/la	replace it
devolver el dinero	return the money

Complaints

NOW	IN THE PAST
los frenos no funcionan the brakes don't work	**la nevera no funcionaba** the fridge didn't work
no hay electricidad there's no electricity	**la playa no existía** the beach didn't exist
nos ha dicho que había un ascensor you told us there was a lift	**no había agua caliente** there was no hot water
está estropeado, -da it's broken down/damaged	**nos había prometido una cocina** you promised us a cooker
	estaba roto, -ta it was broken

Vimos un ratón en el comedor.

2. Informal: To a Friend

You may want to describe a disaster to a friend, perhaps a holiday that went wrong. If you are basing your letter on an advertisement, remember not to use exactly the same words in your account if you can avoid it.

fue un desastre total it was a complete disaster
no te puedes imaginar lo feo que era you can't imagine how ugly it was
el hotel no estaba terminado the hotel wasn't finished
había un olor tremendo por todas partes there was a terrific smell everywhere
veíamos cucarachas en el restaurante y un ratón en el comedor we saw black beetles in the restaurant and a mouse in the dining-room
las comidas eran fatales the meals were appalling
las sábanas estaban sucias the sheets were dirty

estábamos a cinco kilómetros de la playa en vez de cien metros we were 5 kilometres from the beach instead of 100 metres
el pueblo estaba lleno de gamberros the town was full of hooligans
en el bar de abajo, cantaban, gritaban y reían hasta las tres de la madrugada in the bar below, they sang, shouted and laughed until 3 a.m.
después de quejarnos a la guía volvimos a Inglaterra en el primer avión after complaining to the courier, we returned to England on the first plane

Messages

Messages

Usually these consist of about three short sentences. You will need:
perfect tense, for what has happened
present tense, for what is happening now
future tense, for what will happen
a way to tell someone to do something.

Use short, simple sentences. Add nothing extra – you will get no credit and may lose marks. If your answer gives all the information required and would result in the correct action being taken, you get full marks.

Sample Questions

1. *Write a note to your Spanish friend who's staying with you to say you've gone to the cinema with Peter, his supper is in the 'fridge, and you'll be back at 10.30.*

Answer He ido al cine con Peter. Tu cena está en la nevera. Volveré a las diez y media.

2. *While you are alone in your Spanish friend's house, Pilar phones and asks you to give your friend a message to say she's missed the train and will now arrive at 8 p.m. She would like your friend to meet her at the station.*

Answer Pilar ha llamado. Ha perdido el tren y va a llegar a las ocho de la tarde. ¿Quieres ir a buscarla a la estación?

Vocabulary

he dejado las entradas en la mesa
  I've left the tickets on the table
ha olvidado su pasaporte s/he's forgotten her/his passport
no puede llevarte a Cuenca
  s/he can't take you to Cuenca
no puedo verte en la playa I can't meet you on the beach
va a pasar la noche en Segovia
  s/he's going to spend the night in Segovia
te llamaré desde el aeropuerto
  I'll phone from the airport
tendrá que cancelar la cita
  s/he'll have to cancel the appointment
¿quieres avisar al peluquero?
  will you let the hairdresser know?
el reloj está arreglado the watch is mended
los zapatos que pediste han llegado the shoes you ordered have come
puedes recogerlos hoy you can fetch them today
tu abuelo sale del hospital mañana your grandfather's coming out of hospital tomorrow
alguien tiene que ir a buscarle
  someone must fetch him

Ha olvidado su pasaporte.

Telling Someone to Do Something

1. *Quieres* + infinitive   Will you . . . ?
   ¿Quieres telefonearle después de llegar a casa?   Will you phone when you get home?
2. *Tienes que* . . .   You have to . . .
   Tienes que recoger un paquete que ha dejado en el Corte Inglés.
   You have to collect a parcel she left in the Corte Inglés.
3. The imperative – see Chapter 7.

Making Yourself Understood

You should be able to ask for something to be explained, repeated or spelt, and to correct yourself when you say the wrong thing.

¿cómo? pardon? what did you say?	**¿puede repetir, por favor?** could you repeat it, please?
¿qué? what?	**por favor, hable Vd. más despacio** please speak more slowly
¿qué me dice(s)? what did you say?	**me equivoqué** I was wrong, I made a mistake
no comprendo/no entiendo I don't understand	**Vd. se equivoca** you're wrong
¿me entiendes? do you understand?	**¿cómo se escribe?** how do you spell it?
en inglés se dice 'Bless you', en español se dice 'Jesús' in English you say 'Bless you', in Spanish you say 'Jesús'	**se escribe con hache** it's spelt with an 'h'
	deletrear to spell
	es decir in other words
lo que quiero decir es . . . what I mean is . . .	**quiero decir** . . . I mean . . .

– ¿Qué significa 'pronóstico del tiempo'? What does 'pronóstico del tiempo' mean?
– Quiere decir 'weather forecast' It means 'weather forecast'.

– ¿Cómo se dice 'ferret' en español? How do you say 'ferret' in Spanish?
– No lo sé. Explícame lo que es. I don't know. Explain what it is.

Polite Remarks

'Please' and 'thank you' are used less in Spain, so if you thank someone they often reply: *de nada*, 'not at all'; *no hay de qué*, 'it's nothing'.

¡qué aproveche! enjoy your meal	**¡salud!** cheers!
¡enhorabuena! congratulations! (on an achievement)	**es Vd. muy amable** that's very kind of you
¡felicidades! congratulations! (on an anniversary)	**¡adelante!** come in! (said from inside a room)
feliz cumpleaños happy birthday	**pase Vd.** come in (said at the door)
felices Pascuas happy Christmas	**momentito/un momento** just a minute
feliz año nuevo happy New Year	**¡espera!** wait!
¡buen viaje! have a good trip!	
¡suerte! good luck!	

'Lo' + Adjective or Adverb

1. *Lo* + masculine singular adjective is used to express the essential quality of the adjective. The English equivalent is 'the . . . thing'.
   e.g. *Lo malo es que hemos perdido el último autobús.*
   The unfortunate thing is we've missed the last bus.

   Eso es lo más probable.
   That's the most likely thing.

● The adjective is always masculine and singular.

2. *Lo* + adjective + *que es/son* means 'how . . . s/he it is/they are'.
   e.g. *No vas a creer lo perezosos que son.*
   You'll never believe how lazy they are.

   Me pongo la nueva falda, y verás lo bonita que es.
   I'll put on the new skirt and you'll see how pretty it is.

● The adjective agrees with the noun it describes.

3. *Lo* can also be used with an adverb, i.e. *lo* + superlative adverb + *posible* for 'as . . . as possible'.

e.g. *Las necesita lo más pronto posible.*
He needs them as soon as possible.
- *Lo antes posible* and *cuanto antes* also mean 'as soon as possible'.

The Conditional Tense
Formation
Remove the endings from the future tense and add imperfect endings in *-ía*. Thus *hablaré* gives conditional *hablaría; tendré* gives conditional *tendría*.

preguntaría	I would ask
aprenderías	you would learn
decidiría	s/he, you (*Vd.*) would decide
iríamos	we would go
seríais	you would be
sabrían	they, you (*Vds.*) would know

Use
1. The conditional is used as a 'future in the past' in reported speech, when the actual words spoken were in the future tense.

   e.g. *Llegaré lunes.* (future) I shall arrive on Monday.
   (actual words spoken)
   Dijo que llegaría lunes. (conditional) He said he would arrive on Monday.

2. 'If' clauses require a conditional only in certain circumstances.
   a) Present.
   Si viajas en tren, tienes que sacar un billete.
   (present) (present)
   If you travel by train, you must buy a ticket.
   Si los veo, se lo daré.
   (present) (future)
   If I see them, I will give them it.

   b) Past.
   Si ganaba las quinielas, me compraría un coche.
   (imperfect) (conditional)
   If I won the pools, I'd buy myself a car.

Listening Practice
1. In the market one day you see some embroidered blouses. The stallholder is talking to the bystanders.
   a) Why are the blouses a good buy?
   b) What is the advantage of buying this week?

Speaking Practice

2. (Higher level) Listening to the radio, you hear this advertisement.
   a) What is being advertised?
   b) What is offered to attract children?
   c) What flavours are available?
   d) What will your children do if you buy them?

Answers:
1. (a) Machine-washable, don't shrink   (b) 10% discount.
2. (a) Biscuits   (b) A gift in every packet   (c) Lemon, banana   (d) Thank you.

Speaking Practice

1. You are shopping for a present for your sister. The shop assistant speaks to you:

   Can I help you?
   a) Say you're looking for a present.

   Is it for a lady or a gentleman?
   b) Say it's for your sister.

   Does she like pottery?
   c) Say you're not sure.

   What about these scarves?
   d) Ask if they're expensive.

   No — only 200 pesetas.

2. (Higher level)

Situation: You have booked a hired car for your parents while on holiday in Spain. They find the brakes don't work too well, and although you were told the car would be handed over with a full tank, there's only 15 litres of petrol in it. You go to the office of the car-hire company and speak to the receptionist, who is not very helpful.

You must:
   a) Begin the conversation by explaining when you hired the car, and the fact that you expected it to have a full tank of petrol.
   b) Complain about the brakes.
   c) Decide what to do when you receive the reply.

0 Farewell to Spain

This chapter revises eating out, saying 'goodbye', thanking people, expressing pleasure, and complaining in a restaurant. The grammar section revises 'por' and 'para', how to translate 'sitting', the future perfect and conditional tenses and how to suggest something is possible. There are helpful hints on preparing for the speaking test.

Sarah's Farewell

El último día, Sarah se puso muy triste.
—Es que tengo muchas ganas de ver a mi familia ¿sabes?, pero al mismo tiempo os echaré mucho de menos.
—Anímate, Sarah. Te hemos preparado una sorpresa. Esta tarde vamos a ir de tapas, y luego hemos reservado una mesa en el Río Grande, que da al río y tiene unas vistas preciosas de la Torre del Oro y de la Giralda.
—¡Qué bien! ¡Qué sorpresa más maravillosa!

• • • • •

En el restaurante.
—Bueno, Sarah, sírvete tú la primera. ¿Te gusta la salsa? ¿Quieres un poco de ensalada?
—Sí, gracias, es muy buena.
—Pero tómate más, por Dios. No comes nada.
—Que sí, siempre estoy comiendo en España porque me encanta la comida española. Tendré que ponerme a régimen al volver a casa.
—¿Qué te parece el pollo asado? Un poco quemado, ¿no?
—No, no, a mí me parece perfecto.
—¿Quieres más vino, Conchita?
—Gracias, ya tengo suficiente.
—¿Te echo un poquito de agua, Ana?
—Sí, por favor.
—Este pescado es muy rico. ¿Quieres probarlo, mamá?
—Una cucharada, nada más. Delicioso, ¿verdad?
—Oiga, camarero. ¿Nos trae más pan?
—En seguida, señor.

• • • • •

En el aeropuerto.
Buen viaje, Sarah. Escríbenos y vuelve pronto.
—Sí, sí, por supuesto. Pero primero Elena tiene que visitarme en Inglaterra. Lo he pasado estupendamente en Sevilla, y os lo agradezco a todos.

Sarah's Farewell

—De nada, hija. Ha sido una delicia tenerte en casa.
—Sarah, ¿qué es lo que más te ha gustado de España?
—Pues Sevilla es una ciudad encantadora, con el sol, las palmeras, la animación de las calles, los palacios y parques . . . Pero no cabe duda de que lo mejor de España ha sido la gente. Sois tan alegres, tan cariñosos. Un millón de gracias por todo.
—No llores, Sarah. Vuelve a vernos lo más pronto posible. ¿Por qué no vienes por Pascua el año que viene, para la Feria?
—Aquí tienes algunos regalos para tus padres y unos recuerdos de Sevilla para ti. Ponlos en tu maleta antes de facturarla.
—¡Un montón de gracias! ¡Qué amables sois! Adiós y hasta julio, Elena.
—Hasta el año que viene. ¡No te olvides! Te esperamos para la Feria.

Vocabulary

os echaré mucho de menos I'll miss you very much
anímate cheer up
ir de tapas to have snacks with drinks before a meal
tiene unas vistas preciosas it has lovely views
sírvete tú la primera help yourself first
la salsa sauce, gravy
tómate más have some more
me encanta la comida española I love Spanish food
tendré que ponerme a régimen I'll have to go on a diet
al volver a casa when I get home
quemado, -da burnt
ya tengo suficiente I have enough
¿te echo un poquito de agua? shall I pour you a little water?
¿quieres probarlo? do you want to taste it?
una cucharada, nada más just a spoonful
¿nos trae más pan? could you bring some more bread?

vuelve pronto come back soon
lo he pasado estupendamente I've had a marvellous time
ha sido una delicia tenerte en casa it's been a pleasure to have you in the house
¿qué es lo que más te ha gustado de España? what did you like best in Spain?
la animación de las calles the streets full of life
no cabe duda (de que) there's no doubt (that)
¿por qué no vienes por Pascua? why don't you come at Easter?
ponlos en tu maleta antes de facturarla put them in your case before you check it in
¡no te olvides! don't forget!
te esperamos para la Feria we'll expect you for the Fair
despedirse de to say goodbye to
una cena de despedida a farewell dinner

Useful Words and Phrases
Thanking People

un millón de gracias	por todo	a thousand thanks	for everything
un montón de gracias	por una tarde maravillosa	thanks a million	for a wonderful evening
muchísimas gracias	por un día estupendo	very many thanks	for a marvellous day
gracias otra vez	por el regalo	thanks again	for the present

¡cuánto te lo agredezco!	I can't thank you enough!

Expressing Pleasure

¡qué sorpresa más maravillosa! what a wonderful surprise!
¡qué emocionante! how exciting!

cuánto me alegro I'm so glad
me alegro mucho de saber que no hay problema I'm so glad to know there's no problem

Eating Out
In the Bar
(serves continental breakfast, coffee, alcohol, snacks but no meals)

la barra bar counter
el zumo de pomelo grapefruit juice
la sidra cider
una ración de gambas a serving of prawns
    calamares squid
    mejillones mussels
    aceitunas olives
el fino dry sherry
la horchata cold drink made from nuts
los churros doughnut twists
el café café (like bar but with more varied food)
la cafetería a bar serving meals

In the Restaurant

quisiera reservar una mesa para el jueves I'd like to book a table for Thursday
tenemos una reserva a nombre de Pérez we've a reservation in the name of Pérez
el menú del día set meal
el plato combinado meat and vegetables served together
vamos a tomar el menú de 800 pesetas we'll have the set meal at 800 pesetas
los entremeses hors d'oeuvres
el primer plato first course
el postre dessert
frito, -ta fried
asado, -da roast
al horno baked

'Para' or 'Por'

a la plancha grilled	**¿han decidido ya?** have you
el filete de ternera veal steak	**¿han elegido?** decided now?
la carne de vaca beef	**¿y de beber?** what would you like
la chuleta de cerdo pork chop	to drink?
las fresas con nata strawberries	**el vino de la casa** house wine
and cream	**¿es dulce o seco?** is it sweet or
el flan crème caramel	dry?
el pez espada, ¿qué es? what is	**¿con gas o sin gas?** fizzy or still?
swordfish?	**el servicio está incluido** service
¿en qué consiste el gazpacho?	included
what does 'gazpacho' (cold	**el IVA** VAT
soup) consist of?	**quédese con la vuelta** keep the
¿qué recomienda Vd.? what do	change
you recommend?	**la propina** tip

Se ha equivocado en la cuenta.

Complaints

mi amigo no tiene . . .	my friend has no . . .
. . . tenedor	. . . fork
. . . cuchillo	. . . knife
. . . cuchara	. . . spoon
no he pedido cerdo I didn't order pork	
este pescado huele mal this fish smells bad	
se ha equivocado en la cuenta you've made a mistake in the bill	
no hemos tomado agua mineral we didn't have mineral water	
la hoja de reclamaciones the complaints book	

'Para' or 'Por'?

Por gives a reason or cause for the action (referring back); *para* gives a purpose or intention (looking forwards).

e.g. *Trabajaba para mi hermano.* I worked for my brother. (to please him, or he employed me)

Trabajaba por mi hermano. I worked for my brother. (instead of him, because of him)

para	por
1. In order to: Estudió mucho para aprobar. He worked hard to pass.	1. Because of: No aprobó, por ser muy perezoso. He didn't pass because he was very lazy.
2. Why? ¿Para qué compraste el ordenador? Why (for what purpose) did you buy the computer?	2. Why? ¿Por qué compraste el ordenador? Why (because of what, for what reason) did you buy the computer?
3. For: Lo robó para él. She stole it for him. (to give to him)	3. For: Lo robó por él. She stole it for him. (instead of him, because of him)
4. In time for, by: Estará terminado para el martes. It will be finished for (by) Tuesday.	4. For (duration of time): Vamos a Menorca por ocho días. We're going to Minorca for a week.
	5. Through, across, along: El camino pasa por la sierra. The road goes through the mountains. Paseaban por la calle. They were walking along the street.
	6. By: Una novela escrita por Cervantes. A novel written by Cervantes.
	7. In exchange for: Compraron el coche por diez mil pesetas. They bought the car for ten thousand pesetas.
	8. On the occasion of: Me las regalaron por mi cumpleaños. They gave them to me for my birthday.

Useful Phrases

por si acaso	just in case	**por casualidad**	by chance
por eso	therefore	**por desgracia**	unfortunately
por fin	at last	**por ejemplo**	for example
por lo visto	apparently	**por el momento**	for the moment
por todas partes	everywhere	**por primera vez**	for the first time

Sitting

Action

Sentarse is used when someone changes their position from standing up to sitting down.

    e.g. *Se sentaron en el canapé.* They sat down on the sofa.

● The imperfect tense (*me sentaba* etc.) means either that you were in the act of changing to a seated position, or that you kept on changing from standing to sitting down.

Position

For the state of being seated (I am sitting), use *estar* + past participle.

    e.g. *La señora está sentada en el rincón.* The lady is sitting in the corner.

● The past participle agrees with the subject.

Habrán salido.

The Future Perfect
(English 'I shall have . . . -ed')

Formation
The future perfect is formed from the future of *haber* + past participle.
> e.g. *Habremos terminado dentro de una hora.* We shall have finished in an hour.

Use
It is used to suggest probability, referring to a recent event.
> e.g. *Habrán salido.* They've probably gone out/I suppose they've gone out.

The Conditional Perfect
(English 'I would have . . . -ed')

Formation
The conditional perfect is formed from the conditional of *haber* + past participle.
> e.g. *Me habría gustado verlos.* I would have liked to see them.

Use
a) It is used in reported speech, when the actual words spoken were in the future perfect.
> e.g. *Dijeron que habrían terminado dentro de una hora.* They said they would have finished in an hour.

b) It is also used to suggest probability in the less recent past.
> e.g. *Habrían vendido la casa antes de la guerra.* They had probably sold the house before the war.

Probability
Probability can also be expressed by *estar* + gerund.
a) Future of *estar* for present time.
> e.g. *Estará esperando su carta.* He's probably waiting for your letter.

b) Conditional of *estar* for the past.
> e.g. *Estaría esperando su carta.* He was probably waiting for your letter.

The Speaking Test
Role-play
Now
1. Learn by heart the key phrases on each topic.
2. Practise saying them out loud.
3. Invent conversations on the set topics using these key phrases.

In the Examination
1. Use *tú* when speaking to a friend, *Vd.* to an adult who is not a relative.
2. Prepare your role carefully. You are NOT asked to translate, but to make yourself understood by a sympathetic native speaker.
3. Decide what topic is involved; then remember key phrases. Do not translate 'I want you to fill the tank', but rather, think how to buy petrol: *Quiere Vd. llenarme el depósito*, or simply *Lleno, por favor*.
4. Strategies. Sometimes you will forget words. Don't panic.
   a) Say the opposite. You're asked to find out if the castle is open and have forgotten the word for 'open'. *¿El castillo está cerrado?* will get the same information. For 'It's not big enough', say 'It's too small': *Es demasiado/muy/pequeño*.
   b) Find other ways to say it. 'It's expensive' can be *Es caro*, but also *Cuesta mucho* or *Es mucho dinero*.
   c) If desperate, explain. *Las pequeñas frutas rojas* will get some credit if the word 'strawberry' (*fresa*) refuses to come.
5. NEVER use English words.

The Open-ended Role-play (Higher Level)
   a) The examiner may produce a problem you are not expecting, or you may be told to continue the conversation until you reach an agreement. Sometimes you can solve the problem by asking
   ¿Cuál prefieres?   Which do you prefer?
   ¿Por qué no escoges tú el cine?   Why don't you choose the cinema?
   ¿Qué me recomienda Vd.?   What do you recommend?
   ¿Qué regalos tiene . . .   What presents do you have . . .
      . . . *para un niño de diez años?*   . . . for a ten year-old?
      . . . *por mil pesetas?*   . . . for a thousand pesetas?
   b) Learn some phrases for showing agreement.
   Muy bien, me quedo con éste.   All right, I'll take this one.
   De acuerdo.   Agreed, I agree.
   Vale.   Right, OK then.

The Conversation

The examiners decide which topics you must talk about. Your teacher may already have given you a list of questions for which to prepare answers. If not, prepare your own. Remember such topics as money, the weather, transport, and local geography.

a) Avoid answering just *sí* or *no*. The more you say, the less time is left for a difficult topic to arise.
b) It's a conversation – so ask questions, change the subject, answer in incomplete sentences.
c) The exact truth is less important than good Spanish. If your brother is a purser and you don't know the Spanish word, say *trabaja en un barco* or *es marinero*, or even *es camarero*!
d) Give opinions, likes and dislikes.
considero que . . .
a mí me parece que . . . } I think
en mi opinión . . .
supongo que sí/no   I suppose so/not
Express surprise, pleasure, doubt, etc.
e) You can ask for a question to be repeated, say you don't know (*no lo sé, no tengo idea*) or say you aren't interested (*no me interesan los deportes*).
f) Correct mistakes, as you would in English.
   e.g. *Comemos muchos gatos – digo, pasteles*.   We eat a lot of cats, I mean cakes.
g) Think first, then say the whole sentence. Fill the pauses with *pues; bueno; depende; no estoy seguro, -ra*.
h) There are marks for pronunciation and fluency. Record yourself and compare your voice with the Spaniards on the cassette.
   Avoid pronouncing each word separately. The end of one word runs into the next when it begins with a vowel.
   e.g. *las ocho* sounds like *la socho*; *¿cómo está usted?* like *cómo stá sté*.
i) Only topics set by the examiner gain marks, so if your teacher stops you and changes the subject, s/he is only trying to introduce a topic you can gain marks on.

Help Yourself

a) Listen to the question words (*dónde, cuándo*, etc.), and answer the right question.
   e.g. *¿Cómo está?*   How's his health?
        ¿Cómo es?   What's he like?

b) Listen to the <u>tense</u> used, and answer in the same tense. Listen for words indicating past or future time.
e.g. *¿Que <u>hiciste</u> el fin de semana <u>pasado</u>?* What <u>did</u> you do <u>last</u> weekend?
¿Qué <u>harás</u> el fin de semana <u>que viene</u>? What <u>will</u> you do <u>next</u> weekend?
c) Change the pronoun in reflexive verbs – the question will use *te* or *se*, but you reply <u>me</u> *levanto*.
d) Sound confident and speak clearly.
e) Remember, you can't <u>lose</u> marks: they are awarded for what you <u>can</u> say.

Listening Practice

1. You hear an English tourist, Mrs. Robinson, being interviewed on Spanish radio.
    a) What doesn't she like about Madrid?
    b) What's wrong with Spanish food?
    c) What surprises her?

2. (Higher level) In the same programme, a Spaniard who lives on the Costa del Sol is asked his views on tourists in Spain.
    a) What does he say was the first reason tourists came to Spain?
    b) How did Spaniards see them?
    c) Why does he think the British are the worst?
    d) What other things are tourists interested in?
    e) How does he say the typical tourist behaves?

Answers:
1. (a) Too much traffic and pollution   (b) They use a lot of oil, too few potatoes   (c) So many Spaniards speak English.
2. (a) Looking for sun   (b) As a source of income   (c) They spend as little as possible, drink too much, behave badly   (d) Discovering nature, Spanish history and culture   (e) He spends two weeks on the beach and learns nothing of Spain.

Speaking Practice

1. You have been taken out for a meal by your Spanish friend's parents. You are asked:
    Would you like meat or fish?
    a) Say you prefer meat, but you don't mind.

Do you drink wine?
b) Tell him sometimes, but you'd like some mineral water too, please.
Of course. What about a starter?
c) Say you'll have something cold — it's very hot in Seville.
Gazpacho? A salad?
d) Ask him what he recommends.

2. (Higher level) You invite your Spanish friend out for a meal in Madrid. This is the menu.

```
         Restaurante El Caballo Blanco
                   M E N U
                                      Pesetas
         Entradas
         Jamón serrano ................................. 800
         Ensalada andaluza ........................... 300
         Tortilla española ............................. 250

         Sopas
         Gazpacho andaluz ........................... 300
         Sopa del Mediterráneo ..................... 500

         Pescados
         Pez espada al horno ......................... 650
         Boquerones fritos ............................ 600
         Almejas a la marinera ...................... 900

         Carne
         Chuleta de cordero .......................... 750
         Pollo asado ..................................... 450
         Filete de cerdo ................................ 800

         Refrescos
         Aguas minerales .............................. 65
         Colas ............................................. 70
         Cerveza .......................................... 70

         Vinos
         Vino de la casa (tinto, clarete, blanco) .... 150

              Servicio e impuestos incluidos
```

a) Find out what your friend would like.
b) Remember you have only 2500 pesetas to spend.
c) Continue until you have found something you can afford for both of you.

Index of Grammar

a, personal 10
able, to be (can) 100, 101
acabar de 60
adjectives
  agreement 12
  as adverbs 77
  comparative 85
  lo + 112
  meanings change 14
  of nationality 13
  position 14
  possessive 14
  shortened 13
  superlative 86
adverbs
  comparative 85
  formation 76
  irregular 77, 87
  lo + 112
  position 76
  substitutes for 77
  superlative 86
ago (*hace*) 38
agreements
  adjectives 12
  numbers 36
  past participle 89
al + infinitive 53
alphabet 15
apenas, past tense after 102
apocopation (shortened adjectives) 13
article
  + country 59
  neuter *lo* 112
as . . . as 85
auxiliary verb *haber* 89, 102, 121

better, best 87
buen(o) 13, 87
by (*por*) 119

can
  able 100, 101
  know how to 100
cien(to) 36
cold
  people, things, weather 73
commands 90
comparative
  adjective 85
  adverb 85
compound tenses 89, 102, 121

conditional perfect 121
conditional tense 113
conditions (*si*) 113
conmigo etc. 98
conocer 100
continuous
  imperfect 79
  present 38
countries 59
cual(es) 20
cuando
  question 20
  tenses after 53, 102
cuanto 20
¿cuánto tiempo . . . ? 38

dates 36
de after superlative 88
¿de quién? 21
deber 60
deber de 60
descriptions
  people 9
  places 25
desde hace 38
direct object pronouns 99
disjunctive pronouns 98
distance 22
durante = for 38

e for *y* (and) 53
ello neuter pronoun 97
emphasis
  disjunctive pronouns 98
  position of negative 35
  subject pronouns 97
en cuanto, tense after 102
es preciso 61
estar or *ser*? 24
estar + weather 73
  + hot and cold 74

faltar 61
familiar *tú*, *vosotros* 11
for
  desde hace/hacía 38
  llevar 38
  para or *por*? 118
future perfect 121
future tense 46
future after *cuando* 53

gerund (present participle) 39
  + object pronouns 99
going to (future) 46
gran(de) 13
gustar 50

haber 89, 102, 121
haber de 60
habit, imperfect 64, 77
hablar + language 60
hace, ago 38
hace + weather 73, 74
hace/hacía + time 38
hacer falta, to need 61
have just done, to 60
have to, *deber/tener que* 60
hay que 61
hay + weather 73
her
  la 98
  to her *le* 98
him
  le, lo 98
  to him *le* 98
hora 37
hot
  people 73
  things 74
  weather 73, 74

'if' clauses 113
imperative 90
  negative 90
  + object pronouns 91
  reflexive verbs 91
imperfect tense 77
impersonal verbs (*gustar*) 50
'in' after superlative 88
indirect object pronouns 98
infinitive
  al + 53
  + object pronouns 99
-ing 38, 79
ir a + infinitive 46

jamás 35
jugar/tocar 40
just (*acabar de*) 60

know, *conocer/saber* 100, 101

least, the 86
le, les 98
less . . . than 85
like (*gustar*) 50
lo + adjective or adverb 112

llevar (time) 38

mal(o) 13, 87
may I ? 19
mayor/más grande 87

126

mejor 87
menos . . . que 85
mi, tu 14
mí, ti 98
mío, etc. 15
more . . . than 85
most, the 86
must (have to) 60

nada 35
nadie 35
nationality 13
necesitar 61
necessity 60
negative imperative 90, 91
negatives 35
ni . . . ni 35
ni siquiera 35
ningun(o) 13, 35
nosotros 97
nouns, plural 12
nuestro 14
numbers 36
nunca 35

o becomes *u* 53
object pronouns 98
  two third-person 100
  with gerund 99
  with imperative 100
  with infinitive 99
ought to 60

para or *por?* 118
pasar (to stay) 71
passive *se* 19
past participle 88
  agreement 89
  formation 88
  for 'sitting' 120
  irregular 89
past tenses
  imperfect 77
  perfect 88
  pluperfect 102
  preterite 62
  which to use? 64
perfect tense
  formation 88
  object pronouns
    with 89
personal *a* 10
pluperfect tense 102
plural of nouns and
  adjectives 12

poder (can/may) 100
polite commands 90
polite form, you
  (*Vd.,Vds.*) 10
por 118
possessive adjectives 14
present participle –
  see GERUND
present tense 11
preterite tense 62
  irregular forms 63
primer(o) 13
probability 60, 121
progressive tenses
  see CONTINUOUS
pronouns --
  see under type
que 20
quedar 70
querer 101
  = will you? 32, 111
questions 19
quien(es) 20

radical changing verbs
  (stem changing) 12
  imperative 90
  present 12
  preterite 62
reflexive pronouns 18, 98
reflexive verbs
  commands 91
  formation 18
  sentarse, to sit 120

saber 100, 101
se 18, 19, 100
sentarse or *estar*
  sentado? 120
ser or *estar?* 24
shall I? 47
shortened forms 13
should (ought to) 60
si clauses 113
sí, reflexive pronoun 98
since (*desde*) 38
spelling changes in
  preterite 62
stem changes — see
  RADICAL CHANGING
  VERBS
strong pronouns 98
su 14
subject pronouns 97

subjunctive
  avoiding 53
  negative imperative 90
  polite commands 90
superlative 86
suppose 60, 121

tan . . . como 85
tener, expressions
  with 73, 74
tener que 60
tenses
  + emotions 101
  poder/querer/saber 101
  which past? 64
tercer(o) 13
them
  los, las 98
  to them, *les* 98
tiempo (weather) 71
time 37
tocar/jugar 40
tu 98
tú, imperative form 90
  or *Vd.?* 10

u for *o* (or) 53
used to 77
usted, ustedes 10

verbs — see under tense
¿*verdad?* 20
vosotros, imperative 90
vuestro 15

was, were . . . -ing 77, 79
weather 71, 73
when + future time 53
which 20
who 20
will
  future 46, 47
  quieres 32, 111
worse, worst 87
would
  conditional 113
  imperfect 77
  querer 32, 111

y becomes *e* 53
y in numbers 36
ya no 35
year 36
you, familiar and polite
  forms 10

127

Index of Topics

acceptance 33
accidents 83, 85
apologies 34
　replying to 34
application for job 52
approval 50
arranging to meet 34
asking
　questions 19
　the way 22

bank 93
bar 117
breakdown 56
bullfights 42

camping 67
chemist 83
commands 90
complaints
　holiday 108
　restaurants 118
　shop 105
countries 59

daily routine 17
dates 36
dentist 81, 83
describing
　lost property 96
　people 9
　where you live 25
directions 23
disapproval 51
dislikes 51
doctor 81, 82

eating out 115, 117
emotions, tenses with 101
entertainments 41
exchanges 5, 6, 7

filling-station 56
first aid 83
forbidding 32
formal letters
　hotel booking 69
　job application 52
forms 6
free time 40
future plans 44

games, to play 40
garage 56
getting things done 95

hobbies 40
holidays 70
hot and cold 73
hotel, letter to 69

illness 81, 84
informal letters 7, 8
instrument, to play an 40
introductions 34
invitations 31, 33

jobs 44, 96
　letter applying for 52

letters
　formal 52, 69
　informal 7, 8
likes and dislikes 50
listening test
　advice on 54
　practice 15, 28, 42, 55,
　65, 80, 91, 102, 113, 124
lost property 94, 96

making yourself
　understood 111
meet
　arranging to 34
　verbs to use for 40
messages 110
music (to play) 40

necessity 60
notices 27
numbers 36

party planning 31
past tenses
　which to use 64
　with emotions 101
　with *poder, querer,*
　　saber 101
permission 32
play, to
　games 40
　instruments 40
pleasure, expressing 50, 117
polite phrases 112

post office 94
probability 60, 121

quantities 107
questions 19

rail ticket, buying a 57
reading test
　advice on 26
　practice 26, 71
refusals 33
requests 32
restaurant 115, 117
returning purchase 105

school 47, 49
seasons 36
shopping 104, 106, 108
signs 27
sitting 120
skiing 74, 76
Spain compared to
　England 26
speaking test
　advice on 66, 96, 122
　practice 16, 30, 43, 55,
　　65, 80, 92, 103, 114, 124
　practice with hints 66
sport 40
stay (verbs to use for) 70
surprise 52

telephoning 95
tenses
　with emotions 101
　with *poder, querer,*
　　saber 101
　which past? 64
thanks 117
time 37
tourist office 21
town or country? 26
travel and transport 56, 58

understood,
　making self 111

way, asking the 22
weather 71, 73
　forecasts 71
　forecast, questions on 72

128